Agatha Christie:

PLOTS, CLUES AND MISDIRECTIONS

Thirty-three ways the Queen of Crime deceives us

Sally and Tony Hope

The Book Guild Ltd

First published in Great Britain in 2023 by
The Book Guild Ltd
Unit E2 Airfield Business Park,
Harrison Road, Market Harborough,
Leicestershire. LE16 7UL
Tel: 0116 2792299
www.bookguild.co.uk
Email: info@bookguild.co.uk
Twitter: @bookguild

Typeset in 11pt Minion Pro

Printed and bound in the UK by 4edge

ISBN 978 1915853 189

British Library Cataloguing in Publication Data.
A catalogue record for this book is available from the British Library.

To Dr Noboru Maruyama, whose enthusiastic and extensive knowledge of British crime fiction was the origin of a fruitful collaboration and a beautiful friendship.

Acknowledgements

We thank Stewart Tolley and George Breeze for their helpful feedback on an earlier version of this book. We acknowledge with thanks permission from David Higham, agents, to quote from the novel *Unnatural Death* by Dorothy L. Sayers, published by Hodder & Stoughton; and from a lecture that Sayers gave in Oxford in 1935 and that is available online from The Bodleian Library, Oxford. We also acknowledge with thanks permission to quote from *The Gentle Art of Murder: the Detective Fiction of Agatha Christie* by Earl F Bargainnier. [Reprinted by permission of the University of Wisconsin Press. © 2005 by the Board of Regents of the University of Wisconsin System. All Rights Reserved.] Agatha Christie Ltd. refused permission for us to include quotations from Christie's works. On a happier note we are very pleased to be able to thank Dave Hill, Fern Bushnell, Chloe May and all at The Book Guild who have combined efficiency, support and kindness in equal measure. It has been a pleasure working with them all on this book.

Contents

Misdirections

Introduction

Agatha Christie is the biggest-selling novelist of all time. She is author of the longest-running play. The *Poirot* TV series starring David Suchet has been seen by almost a billion people worldwide. These are extraordinary achievements and yet little has been written about her craft. Perhaps her books are just too enjoyable, too popular to be taken seriously as a subject for study. Even Christie's mother-in-law suggested that her talents would be put to better use writing a biography of Shakespeare. That dated distinction between 'high-brow' and 'low-brow' still casts its dark shadow. But Christie's books continue to sell, and each year brings new dramatisations of her works. Christie also inspires others to write in the field she developed: cosy crime and the genuine puzzle whodunnit. It is no coincidence that MC Beaton's detective is called *Agatha* Raisin. *Death in Paradise*, running to at least twelve seasons, is enjoyed by millions, and, like Christie's *A Caribbean Mystery*, combines crime, humour and bright sunshine. Richard Osman's best-seller *The Thursday Murder Club* with its lead detective an extremely sharp elderly woman is more than a nod to Christie's 1927 short story *The Tuesday Night Club* in which the world was first introduced to Miss Marple. The ways in which Christie kept freshly creative for over half a century of writing can inspire us all.

We began reading Christie together when we were medical students. We had been taught anatomical dissection in order to understand how the body works. We applied a similar approach to Christie, examining the structures beneath the surface. We found that the greatest of Christie's deceptions is to give the impression that her writing is simple. It is her genius to seem like the innocent flower yet be the serpent under it. The purpose of this book is to reveal those internal workings: to peel back the surface and show the rich variety of ways in which Christie baffles and mystifies her readers.

This book is the result of reading each of Christie's sixty-six crime novels three times: first for the puzzle, secondly for the craft and lastly for inspiration. We find as much enjoyment in re-reading Christie novels as in the first reading, but the pleasure is different. When we know the solution we can see the cunning ways in which Christie gives the clues whilst hiding them, and how she distracts and deceives. Reading a Christie novel for the second time is like watching a fine craftsman – a furniture maker, for example – at work. The finished piece may look simple but a great deal of skill and artistry have gone into its making. You do not see all the joints, perfectly dove-tailed, that contribute to the stability and elegance, but they are there underneath. For the third time of reading we took the novels in the order in which they were written to see how Christie developed, and continued to refine, her craft.

There are deep parallels between crime fiction and medicine. Christie trained as an apothecary's assistant during the First World War, when she worked in a hospital. It gave her a knowledge of poisons and pharmacology. Conan Doyle, one of Christie's main inspirations, trained as a doctor in Edinburgh. He was taught by Joseph Bell, personal surgeon to Queen Victoria. Bell emphasised the importance of making deductions from the close observation of patients. In Conan Doyle's fecund imagination Bell was transformed into Sherlock Holmes. As medical students we were fortunate in our teachers, too. One was the brilliant diagnostician, Sir John Badenoch. When other consultant doctors were stuck they asked him for help. Badenoch would sit by the bed and invite the patient to tell him their story, from the beginning. He asked only the occasional question. 'If you listen carefully,' he said to us, 'the patient will tell you the diagnosis.' Poirot takes a similar view. He tells us that people will give themselves away when talking on any subject.

Solving a Christie whodunnit is like puzzling out a problematic diagnosis. In a Christie novel there is a truth and a rational explanation. In medicine, too, there is a truth – the diagnosis – and we must not rest until we have found it. Some of what seem to be facts, however, may be distractions, or perhaps deceptions, for the experienced doctor knows that even investigations can deceive. It is our job as doctors to find the clues and to put them together in the right way to make the correct diagnosis, seeing the distractions and deceptions for what they are.

This book is our tribute to Christie. Our aim is to bring into the open what Christie so cleverly kept hidden: the many ways she helps us to the solution of her puzzles whilst, at the same time, deceiving us.

PLOTS

CHAPTER ONE

And then there were two

Re-writing the rule book

No plot spoilers.

Agatha Christie skilfully wove together plot, clues and misdirections to baffle her readers whilst also being fair. Plot is the centrepiece of the whodunnit puzzle. Clues point towards the solution that the plot aims to hide. Misdirections point away from the solution, or conceal the clues.

The most daring way in which Christie used plot to hide the solution was to break with convention: to *re-write the rule book*. In her most original stories she extended the boundaries of the whodunnit. Readers could solve the puzzle only by thinking the unthinkable.

The rules of the whodunnit are somehow created between readers and writers. These generally unwritten conventions allow the author scope and freedom, secure in the knowledge that the reader will understand them. But a great novelist might make use of them in a different way. She might challenge the reader by ignoring the rules.

In a whodunnit this can be particularly powerful: most readers will not consider unconventional solutions.

In 1929 Ronald Knox, a writer of mystery stories and also a Catholic priest, proposed what he called the Ten Commandments of Detective Fiction. Time has shown that these were not written on tablets of stone. The ten commandments were:

1. The criminal must be someone mentioned in the early part of the story, but must not be anyone whose thoughts the reader has been allowed to follow.
2. All supernatural or preternatural agencies are ruled out as a matter of course.
3. Not more than one secret room or passage is allowable.
4. No hitherto undiscovered poisons may be used, nor any appliance which will need a long scientific explanation at the end.
5. No Chinaman must figure in the story.
6. No accident must ever help the detective, nor must he ever have an unaccountable intuition which proves to be right.
7. The detective must not himself commit the crime.
8. The detective must not light on any clues which are not instantly produced for the inspection of the reader.
9. The stupid friend of the detective, the Watson, must not conceal any thoughts which pass through his mind; his intelligence must be slightly, but very slightly, below that of the average reader.
10. Twin brothers, and doubles generally, must not appear unless we have been duly prepared for them.

By 1929 rule 7 – that the detective must not commit the crime – had already been broken, for example in *The Mystery of the Yellow Room* (1907) by French writer, Gaston Leroux – a novel that inspired Christie to write crime fiction. Christie herself had already broken rule 1 – that the criminal must not be someone whose thoughts the reader has been allowed to follow. In fact she had broken that rule in two of her first six novels. In Christie's seventh novel, *The Big Four* (published in 1927) there are several Chinamen and we also meet Poirot's twin brother, Achille. Perhaps Knox did not think much of that novel as a whodunnit – with some justification – and that is why he included Commandment 5. It was not until near the end of her life, when she was in her eighties, that Christie used identical twins to conceal part of the plot. That experiment was not, however, a success.

When Christie started writing in the 1920s, most readers of detective fiction would have had the following expectations:

1. In a first-person narrative the narrator cannot be the murderer.
2. Only a small subset of the suspects can turn out to be the murderers or accomplices.
3. At least some of those who die must have been murdered.
4. The murderer must be a substantial character in the novel.
5. A child cannot be the murderer.
6. There must be motive for the murder of each specific victim: victims cannot be chosen at random.

7. Not all the main characters should die.
8. The principal criminal must have committed the murder or murders.

Christie breaks each of these expectations. She shows again and again that the whodunnit can survive bold innovation. In thinking beyond convention, however, Christie was not adopting an 'anything goes' approach. She was far too precise and logical for that. What she did was to pare back the unwritten rules until there were only two:

1. The author should be fair to the reader in providing the information needed to solve the puzzle; and,
2. The solution should be rational, and must not involve the supernatural (Knox's second commandment).

The first of these rules implies:

1a. The author, in her authorial voice, must not lie to the reader, although any character may lie.

A more stringent version of the second rule might be that the plot and solution are plausible. But what is to count as too implausible? How extraordinary a coincidence, or how unlikely an element of the plot, is acceptable? If an idea has been taken from a true but rare event, is it allowable? Plausibility, we suggest, is not a rule of the genre but, if the solution or plot elements are too implausible, readers may find the novel unsatisfactory.

It is highly desirable not only that the solution be plausible but also that it is the *only* plausible solution that accounts for the key facts. This is not so much a rule of the genre as a feature relevant to the novel's quality. Most whodunnits, including many by Christie, do not have this feature. Whilst a careful writer can make certain that the solution accounts for the key facts, it is difficult to ensure that there is no alternative solution that is also compatible with them.

It is one thing to have the idea for an unconventional plot; it is quite another to bring it off. All of Christie's mould-breaking novels posed difficult narrative problems. Christie solved these with a creative brilliance unmatched by any other whodunnit writer. Occasionally the writing came so easily, for example when writing *Crooked House*, that Christie felt she was simply the scribe. But five out of six novels were for her hard work. Not that she disliked hard work. In her *Autobiography* she suggests that it was the difficulty in planning and writing *And Then There Were None* that she found fascinating.

Christie found the solution to one of the narrative problems posed by the structure of *And Then There Were None* in a child's counting rhyme. In *Murder Is Easy*, published earlier in the same year, she had briefly quoted 'Fiddle de dee, fiddle de dee, the fly has married the bumble bee'. Perhaps nursery rhymes were running in her head when she hit on the idea of using *Ten Little Soldier Boys* to provide both structure and a macabre humour to *And Then There Were None*. Each death is linked to a different verse. The horror is amplified as the relentless countdown continues. The model soldiers on the table mysteriously dwindle in number, as the characters are picked off one by one.

Following the success of *And Then There Were None (1939)*, Christie was rather taken with nursery-rhyme titles. In 1940 she published *One, Two, Buckle My Shoe*. It is possible that this gave her the idea for a clue based on shoes, and the chapter titles follow the lines of the rhyme but they are not relevant to the story. In *Five Little Pigs (1941)*, each of the five main characters, who are all linked to an old, solved murder, has a different personality modelled on one of the little pigs of the rhyme. Each character gives a different, yet overlapping, version of the same events. *Crooked House* (1949) is about a family living together in a metaphorically crooked house, but the nursery rhyme is not otherwise relevant. In *A Pocket Full of Rye* (1953) the murders seem connected with the rhyme but, in stark contrast with *And Then There Were None*, the connections are forced and unconvincing. The tail seems here to be wagging the dog. In *Hickory Dickory Dock* (1955) the action takes place in a house in Hickory Road. The name was chosen to justify the title. The rhyme, however, is irrelevant to the story.

And Then There Were None has sold more than any other of Christie's books: over one hundred million copies. The strange thing is that it is not primarily a *whodunnit*. Unlike in the majority of her crime novels there is little attempt to provide clues. At the denouement three clues are mentioned, but they are so arcane, and one purely symbolic, that they can hardly be considered clues at all. What Christie did in this highly original book was to combine features of the whodunnit, the locked-room mystery and the thriller to construct a novel that was all her own.

Four years before *And Then There Were None* Christie published *The A.B.C. Murders.* If there is any whodunnit plot that should be beyond the pale then this surely is it: a serial killer carrying out random killings.

CHAPTER TWO

The motiveless motive

Rational reasons for random killings

Plot spoilers for: *Endless Night*; *The A.B.C. Murders*.

> *Some are born to Sweet Delight*
> *Some are born to Endless Night*
> ['Auguries of Innocence' by William Blake]

One of the unwritten rules of the whodunnit that Christie broke was that *there must be motive for the murder of each specific victim: victims cannot be chosen at random*. It is unsatisfactory in a whodunnit if the murderer is simply a psychopath – if the reason for the murders is only the love of killing.

In her darkest book, *Endless Night* (1967), Christie explores the mind of a psychopath. This novel is a long way from the cosy crime for which she is famous. The reader has no doubt, from the beginning, that Michael Rogers, the narrator, is born to Endless Night. He tells us that he enjoys killing – it makes him happy. Christie was in her late seventies when she wrote this. She was still exploring different types of novel: different ways of writing. *Endless Night* is not a whodunnit. It is Christie's version of Nordic noir.

The idea of the *psychopath* has had a long and chequered history in both forensic psychiatry and in literature. If used at all in modern psychiatry it refers to a diffuse grouping of various types of antisocial behaviour together with a lack of normal emotional responses such as remorse. In literature the psychopathic murderer, often superficially charming, may kill for no reason other than the love of killing, and may go on killing. Psychopaths are popular in thrillers: they are the epitome of evil.

Endless Night is unique amongst Christie's novels. She wrote many adventure thrillers (several starring Tommy and Tuppence) but the thrill in these is in the danger to the lead characters, not in the psychology of the killer. In several novels there are scenes, but only scenes, that give a feeling of eerie malevolence – Gwenda's exploration of the house near the beginning of *Sleeping Murder* (1976), for example. In *And Then There Were None* (1939) there is a sense of evil throughout the novel, but that is created by the setting and the story, not by character.

Creative people will often build on what they have previously achieved, reusing elements but in new ways. This is what Christie did in *Endless Night*. It was, for her, a new type of novel, but in choosing the narrative perspective she borrowed from *The Murder of Roger Ackroyd* (1926), and part of the central plot is from *Death on the Nile* (1937). Creative people, of course, also beg, borrow and steal from others. It has been suggested that

in writing *The Murder of Roger Ackroyd* Christie may
have borrowed a significant element from *Jernvognen*.
Jernvognen, published in 1909, is by the Norwegian writer
and journalist, Kristoffer Elvestad Svendsen using the
pen name Stein Riverton. This novel was translated into
English, as *The Iron Chariot*, by Lucy Moffatt in 2017. It is
an early example of Nordic noir. Much of the interest, as in
Dostoevsky's *Crime and Punishment*, is the psychological
disintegration of the criminal as the detective closes in.
It is unlikely that Christie knew about *Jernvognen*, and
in any case, unlike *The Murder of Roger Ackroyd*, it is not
a whodunnit. If one is looking for a Christie parallel for
Jernvognen then *Endless Night* is a much better example.

Endless Night is not the only Christie to include a
psychopathic killer. In *By the Pricking of My Thumbs* (1968)
the murderer is an assassin who starts to go mad. Christie
was almost eighty years old when she wrote this and it is
one of her least satisfactory whodunnits. In several novels,
for example in *Lord Edgware Dies* (1933) and *Hickory
Dickory Dock* (1955), the killers show psychopathic traits
but these books work as whodunnits because the motives
for the murders are nothing to do with the psychopathy. In
Curtain (1975), however, the perpetrator enjoys murder
and is *not* motivated by any of the classic whodunnit
desires. And yet *Curtain* is a very good whodunnit. How
does Christie manage this? The key is that the central
plot idea is brilliant, and, in the context of a whodunnit,
original. In addition the psychological motivation of the
perpetrator is developed so that although it is not based on
a classic desire it is not hidden from the reader. Crucially,

Christie provides good clues to both the central idea and the motivation. Readers who hit on the solution will be sure that they have done so, and yet it is not obvious. *Curtain* is one of the novels in which Christie hides the solution with a plot that breaches convention.

The A.B.C. Murders (1936), however, is Christie's serial-killing masterpiece. The question she set herself was whether it is possible to write a satisfying whodunnit which appears to be about a serial killer, killing at random. Christie had an ability, when needed, to find a dramatic structure in which to set her puzzles. This might be a macabre counting rhyme (*And Then There Were None*), or theatrical performance (*Three Act Tragedy*). In *The A.B.C. Murders* it is the alphabet. The random murders are not quite random. The first victim is Alice Ascher from Andover. The second, Betty Barnard of Bexhill. The third, Carmichael Clarke from Churston.

The motive for these unconnected killings, it turns out, is simple and has nothing to do with psychopathy. What is not simple is how to tell the story. One problem Christie faced was how to keep the suspects for each murder as characters throughout the story given that each murder is unrelated to the others. The second major problem is how to write a red-herring plot that provides a suspect whilst hiding the solution.

Christie solved the first problem by creating a group of people, a kind of posse, made up of key suspects from the first three murders, who set themselves the task, under the direction of Poirot, of finding the 'mad' murderer. To solve the second problem Christie did something pretty innovative. She created a character, with the absurd, but dramatically appropriate, name, Alexander Bonaparte Cust, and devoted eight of the thirty-five chapters to him, chapters that are quite separate from Hastings' narrative. In the reader's mind Cust is readily identified as the 'mad' murderer.

Christie would have been rightly unhappy with the creation of Cust had he remained unconnected to the murderer's plot: it would have been too much of a coincidence for him to be near the scene of each of the crimes. So the final piece in Christie's solution to her authorial puzzle is for the murderer to set up the unsuspecting Cust as fall guy. The solution is satisfying because there is a perfectly rational explanation for the bizarre killings and a classic motive.

Towards the end of *The A.B.C. Murders* Poirot suggests that Cust is like the fox and the murderer like the English hunt. Poirot finds fox-hunting a strange and cruel sport. He castigates Hastings, the conventional Englishman, for being about to suggest that the fox enjoys the chase. But even worse for the fox than death, Poirot suggests, is to be kept captive. The death penalty, Poirot, and perhaps Christie, is suggesting is at least preferable to life imprisonment.

The A.B.C. Murders was not the first of Christie's books in which there is a rational reason for a random killing. She had already carried out what a scientist might call a *pilot experiment*. One year previously she wrote *Three Act Tragedy*. In that novel there is poison in a cocktail glass but the murderer has almost no control over who drinks from the glass: a kind of Russian roulette. At the end of the novel, after the denouement, Poirot is talking with his friend Mr Satterthwaite. Satterthwaite suddenly realises that he himself might have drunk from the poisoned glass. Poirot tells him that there is an even worse possibility: the victim could have been Hercule Poirot.

CHAPTER THREE

Plenty of nothing

What appears to be valueless might be priceless

Plot spoilers for: *Sad Cypress*; *After the Funeral*; *A Pocket Full of Rye*; *They Came to Baghdad*.

Christie breached convention in half a dozen or so novels. Each is a classic of detective fiction. But there are only so many conventions to breach. For most of her whodunnits she had to find other ways in which to use plot to hide the solution. One way is to conceal the motive.

As we have seen, in a few of Christie's novels the killings appear to be random – without motive. In most Christie whodunnits, however, the principal motives are the big four: money or status, revenge, love, and fear of the discovery of a previous crime. There is, by the way, a sexual disparity amongst Christie's murderers. When a man and woman are working together the man is usually motivated by money but the woman by love. Such is life, or death.

The plot in many a thriller involves a valuable object that has gone missing, and may be hidden. In Christie's early novel, *The Secret of Chimneys* (1925) the characters search high and low for the fabulous Koh-i-Noor diamond (the name means Mountain of Light) that has been stolen. It might be secreted in the Tudor mansion, *Chimneys*. The novel has elements of the gothic with secret passages, an enormous library and suits of armour. The thrill in this book is the breathless chase. In *Cat Among the Pigeons* (1959) there are again hidden jewels. This time the jewels are hidden in a portable and seemingly innocent item. An apparently almost worthless object contains enormous wealth. The novel is well clued and very funny.

Between these two novels Christie experimented in various ways with items of hidden value. In her adventure story *They Came to Baghdad* (1951), we know that a spy is carrying information but we do not know how. It turns out that the scruffy red knitted scarf that the dying spy is holding to his wounded chest has the secret code knitted into its pattern. The young woman who finds him throws the scarf into her suitcase and forgets all about it. No one searching her luggage would look at it twice. Once its secret is understood, however, this valueless scarf becomes priceless.

Christie uses this idea of hidden value in some of her whodunnit plots. As so often she rings the changes. In *Sad Cypress* (1940) one of the victims, Mary Gerrard, has the legal right to a fortune, but she does not know it. Everyone except the murderer believes that she is poor. It appears that no one could gain financially from her death. So we look elsewhere for motive, and it is easy to find. Jealousy. Roddy had been engaged to Elinor but jilted her when he falls in love with Mary. So Elinor is arrested. Inspector Marsden is confident that he has identified the killer and the motive. He is wrong, however, and it takes some time, and the clue of the thornless rose, before Poirot, whilst giving evidence in the witness box, can reveal the true murderer, like a conjuror pulling rabbits out of a hat.

In *After the Funeral* (1953) it is the murderer alone who knows the value of what seems valueless. Two members of the Abernethie family die in rapid succession. Richard Abernethie and a short while later his sister, Cora. Richard was immensely rich. His death will benefit his family, all of whom are desperate for cash. Cora, his sister, was not rich. After Richard's funeral, Cora suggests that Richard Abernethie was murdered. By implication she could identify his killer. So when, the next day, Cora is found dead it looks as though the murderer of Richard Abernethie must have killed her. There is no other motive. Cora had plenty of nothing. Or so it seems.

A Pocket Full of Rye (1953) is one of Christie's more contrived books themed around a nursery rhyme. A man buys *The Blackbird Mine*, in East Africa, as a speculation. Over the years it turned out to be completely worthless. The man and various other people are murdered with no obvious motive. The murderer alone, amongst the characters in the book, knows significant deposits of uranium have just been found in the mine. The apparently valueless mining rights are now worth a fortune. *After the Funeral* was published nine months before *A Pocket Full of Rye*. Christie was thinking about the plot theme of 'plenty of nothing' and exploring ways to use it. She enjoyed mining her rich seam of plot possibilities. It is intriguing that Poirot is the detective in *After the Funeral*, and Marple in *A Pocket Full of Rye*. Perhaps Christie thought that although the bones of the plots are the same, changing the detective would give a different feel to the two novels.

CHAPTER FOUR

Missing the target

Concealing the intended victim

Plot spoilers for: *Towards Zero*; *Peril at End House.*

Ariadne Oliver is a writer of detective stories and a friend of Hercule Poirot. In *Cards on the Table* (1936) she says that all the thirty-two novels she has written are really exactly the same. Christie's books, unlike those of Ariadne Oliver, are all different. Like most creative artists, however, she repeats elements. One of her favourite plot devices for hiding motive was to conceal the identity of the intended victim.

Poirot tells us that the dead lips of the victim will name the murderer if only we take the trouble to listen. After the first murder in a whodunnit we ask ourselves: who has motive to kill that particular person? In a few of Christie's novels neither the reader nor the detectives know the identity of the dead body until near the end of the story. These novels highlight the difficulty of discovering the murderer without a knowledge of the victim. Christie developed this thought further. Consider a plot in which it looks as though the intended victim is A when in fact she is B. The reader is likely to join the detectives on a wild goose chase, misunderstanding the murderer's motive and giving thought to the wrong suspects. Christie, with characteristic creative energy, explored many variations on concealing the intended victim.

In one novel the murderer fakes his own death. There are further killings. Since the reader believes the actual murderer is a victim, he is not a suspect. You focus on all the people still alive, to try and guess which one must be the murderer. In another novel a murder goes wrong. The best-laid schemes of mice and murderers occasionally go agley. In that novel the person who drinks the poison was not the intended victim. And so the reader from the beginning is looking for a motive for the wrong death.

In many crime novels the first murder is followed by further murders. The motive for these further deaths is that the victims know the identity of the murderer. It is the motive for the first murder that will help the reader identify the perpetrator. Christie plays on this assumption. In one novel it is the second murder that provides the key to the motive. Although the first murder is connected with the second murder any attempt to find a motive only leads the reader astray. In an even more radical plot the key murder is hidden amongst many murders: a smokescreen that conceals the true motive.

For most of Christie's career the punishment in the UK for murder was death by hanging. This provided her with a particularly subtle way of concealing the intended victim: person A is killed in order to frame person B for the murder. The murderer wishes to see person B publicly humiliated in court, and then hanged. Although person A is a victim, her death is simply a means to an end. The main intended victim is B. Thus the main murder suspect, B, is, in fact, the intended victim: a neat plot trick.

Christie uses this plot in *Towards Zero* (1944). It did not, it seems, come from nowhere. She had worked towards it by stretching the boundaries of her plots like an expert pizza cook stretching the dough. In *Sad Cypress* (1940) a woman is on the verge of being found guilty of murders she did not commit. In *Five Little Pigs* (1943) an innocent woman is found guilty of murder, and dies in prison. The police got the wrong person, and the real murderer keeps quiet. It may have been in thinking about these victims of the criminal justice system that Christie conceived the idea of the perpetrator purposely framing an innocent person as revenge.

In one of Christie's most elegant plots the murderer herself appears to be the intended victim. The murderer arranges things so that it looks as if the person killed was killed in error. This clearly appealed to Christie because it is the central plot idea in three of her novels – all of them first-rate whodunnits. The first was *Peril at End House* (1932). Poirot and Hastings are together on holiday. A bullet strikes the wall behind them, just missing a beautiful young woman, Nick Buckley. Nick tells Poirot that she has had three previous near-death escapes. Poirot and Hastings valiantly spring to the aid of this innocent maiden in distress, and vow to protect her. They meet her rather unsavoury, immoral friends. Poirot begs Nick to invite her cousin, Maggie Buckley, to stay with her, as protection. Maggie accepts the invitation and is then tragically shot, apparently being mistaken for Nick.

Christie uses this plot device in two later novels which share not only the central idea but also one of the main red-herring plots. It is almost as though the second novel is a re-write of the first. It is not surprising that Christie occasionally repeats major aspects of plot given she wrote sixty-six crime novels – what is impressive is her variety. Nevertheless it could be considered a weakness. Or not. There is a different perspective.

Many creative artists repeat themselves. Repetition is perhaps a feature of creativity. Monet painted over thirty pictures of Rouen Cathedral: the same central subject but each time in a different light. Handel's wonderful aria 'Lascia ch'io pianga' (Let me weep) began as an unsung sarabande in an opera written in 1705. In 1707 he repurposed the melody for an aria in an oratoria with the words 'Lascia la spina' (Leave the thorn). In 1711 he again used the melody this time in his opera *Rinaldo*. This is the aria that is now so often performed in the concert hall and out of its operatic context. Although the melody remained the same the setting and the words developed. Each iteration was different, although they share the same tune.

Yehudi Menuhin recorded the same piece of music – the Elgar Violin Concerto – twice with the same conductor – Adrian Boult. It is estimated that there are more than two thousand covers of the Beatles' song *Yesterday*. No one suggests that such repetition is valueless on the grounds that each is a version of the same essential core. On the contrary, we value the fact that there can be different interpretations of the same piece of music.

The three Christie novels in which the murderer appears to be the intended victim share, of course, the same central plot. But they are variations on that theme. The characters, the settings, the humour, the social observations are very different. And so are some elements of plot. In one the murder is carefully planned some time in advance. In another it is almost spontaneous – quickly improvised following an unwitting revelation. Christie weaves quite different cloths using the same central pattern.

What Christie neatly demonstrates is that you cannot afford to have any assumptions. The dead may be the murderers. The murderer may be an innocent victim. The dead may not be dead. The dead may not be who they seem to have been. If they really are dead, and correctly named, they may or may not be the intended target. The moral of this tale: in a Christie you have to keep a high index of suspicion – about everything.

CHAPTER FIVE

Did he jump or was he pushed?

Even in crime novels not all deaths are murders

Plot spoilers for: *Taken at the Flood*; *After the Funeral*.

It is a truth universally acknowledged that a death in a whodunnit is murder, even when in want of motive or means. The watchful reader views any suicide, accident or peaceful death with the utmost suspicion.

There are a few genuine accidents in Christie novels, such as the one at the start of *The Man in the Brown Suit* (1924), when our heroine is waiting at Hyde Park Corner tube station. Suddenly a man near her on the platform appears to recognise someone, reels backwards in terror and falls onto the electric rails. This chap was not pushed, nor did he mean to jump, but he did die. Poirot himself is nearly killed by a train in *Mrs McGinty's Dead* (1952) when he *is* pushed from behind. He is rescued in the nick of time by the quick reflexes of a kind stranger. It seems odd that so few of Christie's murderers follow the obvious strategy of trying to kill the Belgian with the vast quantity of little grey cells. The closest to a successful assassination attempt is in *The Big Four* (1927) when Poirot and Hastings are blown up.

Christie, of course, tricks us with twists on the 'universally acknowledged truth'. Although usually an apparent suicide or natural death turns out to be murder, just occasionally an apparent murder turns out to be suicide, or an accident, or a natural death. Christie first attempted this ruse, a suicide masquerading as murder, in *Murder in the Mews* (1937), a short novella. Even the title is a misdirection. Christie then ran with this idea in her full-length novel, *Taken at the Flood* (1948).

Taken at the Flood is one of Christie's most miserable whodunnits. No character in the book, except Poirot, is kind or pleasant. It is a bitter post-war read. Christie's son-in-law, Hubert, was in the Royal Air Force and had been reported missing in action in France in August 1944. His death was confirmed the following October leaving Christie's daughter, Rosalind, a war widow at twenty-five years of age, with their baby, Matthew. Christie spent time supporting Rosalind and helping to look after her only grandchild. It is no coincidence that the Blitz blast that kills the millionaire at the start of the story took place in October 1944 – the same month that Hubert's death was confirmed. The humour, which normally makes Christie's writing so enjoyable a read, has been extinguished in this novel by very personal grief.

Taken at the Flood has one of the most complicated alibis in any Christie book. The reason for the convoluted alibi is that Hunter, who was a commando in the war and is reckless and fearless, discovers a body. The dead man had been blackmailing him. Hunter had arranged to meet him, to pay him a sizable amount of cash. The landlady overhears the conversation between Hunter and the blackmailer. Hunter is smart enough to realise that in the eyes of the police he will be their prime murder suspect. Hunter disguises the time of the death, making it seem that the blackmailer was still alive later that night. This allows Hunter time to establish his alibi while the dead man would be assumed to be alive. Innocent people don't need alibis. The police arrest Hunter for murder, as he is their only suspect, but eventually he is released when his alibi appears to be true. The main plot of the book is the hunt for the murderer of the blackmailer. At the end of the book, however, it is revealed that no murder took place. The blackmailer was accidently killed. Someone else wished to frame David Hunter for murder.

In *Taken at the Flood* there are also two apparent suicides. One really is suicide but the suicide note is removed because it incriminated the person who finds the dead body. The other suicide really is murder. It is a complex plot. Rosaleen is one of the main characters: a young war widow. Through the story you have glimpses that Rosaleen's conscience is deeply troubled. When she is found dead in bed there is a suicide note in her handwriting. The post-mortem, however, shows a fatal morphine dose was substituted for her mild sleeping draught. Poirot tracks down her murderer by a hunch rather than with the help of clues. Christie uses her ingenuity to weave all three deaths into a hangman's noose.

After the Funeral (1953) provides a much more subtle example of a natural death appearing to be murder. The wealthy Richard Abernethie has died, apparently from natural causes. At the gathering after his funeral, however, his sister, Cora, suggests that her brother was murdered, to the consternation of her relatives and friends. Cora loves saying outrageous things and then sitting back and watching the reaction. When Cora is found murdered the next day everyone, including the reader, assumes that Cora was right and that Richard Abernethie's murderer has killed her. In fact, Richard died of natural causes, and Cora chose to make this outrageous accusation for motives of her own.

CHAPTER SIX

Deception and the doctor

Masking the means of murder

Plot spoilers for: *The Mysterious Affair at Styles*; *4.50 from Paddington*.

Motive, means and opportunity: the solution must account for all three. We have seen how Christie uses plot to mask motive. She also devised plots to mask the means by which victims meet their death.

No one is better placed to mask the means of murder than the doctor. Better even than masking the means is to hide the murder altogether under the guise of suicide or natural causes. In the 1920s family doctors were often single-handed rather than working in large practices as we do now. They knew their patients well, often visiting them at home, as we did too, although this practice is now disappearing. In the early Christie novels family doctors even carry out post-mortem examinations, which would be unthinkable today. We might, for all these reasons, expect doctors to feature prominently as murderers. A friend said to us that in a Christie novel 'it's always the doctor who did it'. But this is not true. In the majority of her novels in which a doctor is a possible suspect he turns out to be innocent. Most of Christie's doctors, however, are not even suspects. They are either innocent bystanders or are duped into writing a death certificate they should not have issued, or into misidentifying the cause or time of death.

Agatha Christie's training as an apothecary's assistant gave her a superb understanding of poisons and of the possible toxic consequences of medicines. In her first published novel, *The Mysterious Affair at Styles* (1920), she uses this knowledge, rather than a doctor's privileged position, to mask the means of murder.

In 1920 in England you could buy strychnine over the counter if you gave a valid reason! In Christie's novel the murderer's accomplice, disguised, buys strychnine from the local chemist. A short while later the lady of the house is fatally poisoned by strychnine. The assumption is that the poison that killed her is the poison bought from the chemist. The real source of the strychnine, however, turns out to have been entirely different. With the means and method of the poisoning hidden, the murderer slips behind his mask into the shadows: the doctor and the reader are fooled.

Christie's plot in this first novel depends on some rather esoteric pharmacology that we could not possibly be expected to know, even as doctors. In the 1920s some prescribed tonics contained small quantities of soluble strychnine. These tonics were not dangerous because the concentration of strychnine was low. Only very small amounts of this medicinal liquid were consumed at any one time. If potassium bromide, then widely used as a sedative, is added to a solution containing dissolved strychnine, the strychnine precipitates out, falling to the bottom of the bottle. The last sip from a bottle of tonic to which the bromide has been added will contain a fatal quantity of precipitated strychnine.

As Christie's confidence grew she moved away from plots influenced by Conan Doyle (chapter 12). Sherlock Holmes impresses the reader with his vast knowledge. We gasp and admire from afar, but we do not engage with his thinking. Christie developed her own style, with clues that the reader can put together to solve her puzzles.

The source of a fatal poison is again masked in Christie's 1957 novel *4.50 from Paddington*. This time it *is* the doctor who did it, and he uses his privileged position to carry out the murder. He puts a small amount of arsenic into a cocktail jug. The Crackenthorpe family drink the cocktails. Later that evening, since he is the family doctor, he is called back when all the family are taken ill, although not fatally so. He uses this opportunity to do two things: kill one of the family members with an extra dose of arsenic, and sprinkle arsenic in the remains of the curry eaten at supper. This deceives everyone into thinking that the curry was the source of the fatal poison. The suspects appear to be only those in the house at the time the supper was cooked and then served. This is a double misdirection masking both the means and the timing of the murder. Unlike in *The Mysterious Affair at Styles* the reader needs no knowledge of pharmacology, but just a deep suspicion of everybody, and the imagination to see how the crime could have been committed.

In the perfect murder no one realises that the death is a murder. By avoiding the police investigation, the murderer gets away with – well – murder. There are two ways this happens in a Christie plot. The first is by curating the murder to look like a suicide. There are several examples in Christie's novels. The second is to make the death look natural or accidental (chapter 5). Both these often fool Christie's family doctors, who simply certify the death, and dash off to the next home visit. We, of course, are not usually fooled. Is there a perfect murder in any Christie novel? Just one. In *Curtain* (1975) there is such a brilliant murder, concealed as suicide, that the police are never involved. The coroner brings in a suicide verdict. Case closed. There is, of course, only one man who could bring this off – who is clever enough to fool everyone else and conceal a murder as a suicide.

Murders that look as though they are natural deaths tend to involve the elderly or frail. They are expected deaths. In *Dumb Witness* (1937) an elderly frail lady who has had a previous episode of jaundice dies quietly in bed. Her family doctor thinks the death is natural and issues the death certificate. She is buried in the local churchyard. We know better because the lady was immensely rich and, just before her demise, she had consulted Poirot. She thought that one of her family was trying to kill her. Poirot promises to be discreet in order to uphold the family honour. He is so discreet that the police are never involved.

In *By the Pricking of My Thumbs* (1968), the doctor confides to Tommy Beresford (the Tommy of Tommy and Tuppence) that he thinks several residents in an old people's home have died from an overdose of morphine. The doctor has no idea how many as he doesn't want to tell the police and cause a scandal! Tommy, Tuppence and the doctor all agree to hush it up. The result is, to a modern reader, quite shocking: the person who has killed many children and countless old people is not brought to justice. The victims' families never learn who was the killer or even, in some of the cases, that their relatives had been murdered.

Morphine was, and still is, used as a pain-killer. Sleeping pills are much more widely prescribed than morphine and until the 1970s barbiturates were the most widely used sedatives. With barbiturates there is a narrow range between the useful and the fatal doses. With the development of safer alternatives they are no longer prescribed by family doctors. Marilyn Monroe died from a barbiturate overdose in 1962. There is still controversy about her death over half a century later, with conspiracy theorists having a field day. This narrow range of dose provided Christie with plots where people die from an overdose of *prescribed* barbiturates: murders masquerading as suicide or accident.

In *The Pale Horse* (1961), despite being in her seventies, Christie comes up with yet another way of masking the means of murder, though it does, as with her first novel, draw on some rather specialised knowledge of poisons. The *Pale Horse* of the title is a former pub which is part of a business that will perform contract killings. The means of death are carefully masked and one of the puzzles for the reader is how these killings can appear to be natural deaths. The mechanism of death is said to be brought about by witchcraft, but of course, in an Agatha Christie, that cannot be the case. Two brave young adventurers decide to take on the forces of evil.

One of the cleverest murders that appears as a natural death is in *Towards Zero* (1944). *Towards Zero* is different from Christie's usual fast-paced tracking down of the murderer. It is a 'slow burn' with many apparently unconnected story lines in the first half. Despite our usual assumption that all deaths are murders, Christie fooled us, as well as the doctor in the book. We thought that one murder was a natural death. Treves, an old lawyer in his eighties, witters on about people from previous murder cases decades ago. He has severe heart disease. He is on holiday by the seaside but requires a hotel with a lift, as stairs will be fatal for his angina – this was in 1944, long before the development of highly effective treatments for angina, such as coronary artery bypass grafting. After a tedious dinner party, Treves potters back to his hotel, and is found dead in bed in the morning. The doctor writes out the death certificate as a clear case of acute on chronic heart disease. The lift was broken, and poor Treves had had to take the stairs. Only later we find out the lift was not broken. Someone had put an 'Out of Order' sign on it specifically to kill Treves.

Earlier in the novel Treves made an interesting observation about detective fiction. Novels usually begin with the murder but for Treves the murder is the end. The interesting story, for Treves, is the story of how the causes and the characters involved all converge to bring about what he calls Zero Hour – the moment of the murder.

Christie may have had Treves' criticism in mind when, almost twenty years later, she wrote *Endless Night*.

CHAPTER SEVEN

Men were deceivers ever

Unlikely partners in crime

Plot spoilers for: *The Mysterious Affair at Styles*; *Death on the Nile*; *Evil Under the Sun*; *Taken at the Flood*.

> *Sigh no more, ladies, sigh no more.*
> *Men were deceivers ever,*
> *One foot in sea, and one on shore,*
> *To one thing constant never.*
> [*Much Ado about Nothing* by William Shakespeare]

One of the most flexible plot devices that can be used to hide motive or opportunity is the use of partners in crime.

Christie and Shakespeare portray intelligent, feisty women who put themselves out for their men, like Portia in *The Merchant of Venice*, or Tuppence for Tommy Beresford in their various Christie adventures. Both also write about men and women who deceive others – in an equal opportunity way. Sometimes it is the man who is the prime mover and a besotted woman his accomplice.

In other plots it is the woman who masterminds the crime, and a chap who does her bidding with dog-like devotion. In Shakespeare the audience is usually in the know about the deceiving couple from the beginning, like Lady Macbeth goading Macbeth to murder the King to gain the crown. In Christie books the reader is kept in the dark. You have to be alert to subtle clues; the most unlikely people may be in league with each other.

Christie sets the tone in her very first whodunnit, *The Mysterious Affair at Styles* (1920). A rich, middle-aged woman is poisoned. From the start her husband, Mr Inglethorpe, is the obvious suspect. A bit too obvious. The reader is suspicious. Then Poirot appears to prove that he is not the murderer. From then on the reader is led away from suspecting him. For this plot to work the murderer needed an accomplice, but Inglethorpe is an unpleasant loner. Christie uses several techniques to mislead us. The personality of Miss Howard, the accomplice, seems to be unlike that of a ruthless killer. She is a hearty, down-to-earth, slightly rough spinster with a heart of gold, and very much attached to Mrs Inglethorpe, the victim. Miss Howard pretends to loathe the murderer, and appears to try to get him convicted of murder. This is a bluff. Miss Howard and Mr Inglethorpe are working secretly together. They hide their mutual passion from the other household members. When Hastings suspects her, Poirot counteracts Hastings' reasoning. We look at the other family characters as suspects, and are fooled.

Over the next fifty years, and in nineteen novels, Christie uses unlikely pairings of deceiving men and women working together as the backbone for plots. Passions, whether love or hatred, seem easy emotions to assume in order to fool other characters and the reader into discounting two people as a lethal unit. In *Death on the Nile* (1937) almost every character deceives, from the crooked American lawyer – there's a shock – to the angry English communist. There are two separate groups of jewel thieves, a terrorist, and cold-blooded murderers. Most whodunnits by most authors have no more than one or two decent clues. *Death on the Nile*, written by Christie at the height of her powers, has at least eleven separate clues to point you in the correct direction. The story is simple. Linnet Ridgeway is the golden girl: beautiful, clever and worth millions. Everyone admires and loves her, or at least keeps their envy and malice well hidden. Jacqueline de Bellefort, Linnet's best friend from schooldays, has no money. The handsome Simon Doyle is engaged to Jacqueline but is also impoverished. They want money in order to get married so Jacqueline brings Simon to meet Linnet, begging her friend to give him a job. A few months later Simon breaks his engagement to Jacqueline and marries Linnet. The happy couple go off down the Nile for a honeymoon cruise. The only problem is that Jacqueline de Bellefort, fuelled by righteous indignation at the treachery of her best friend and her ex-fiancé, becomes the stalker from hell. Where Linnet and Simon go hand in hand, Jacqueline is there to spoil it by creating an unpleasant scene. And then, Linnet Doyle is murdered.

Christie writes a classic piece of misdirection. Hercule Poirot draws up meticulous lists of those with a motive for killing Linnet Doyle, and those free from suspicion. The only two passengers on board the Karnak steamer not on either list are Jacqueline de Bellefort and Simon Doyle. They have watertight alibis. But, in a Christie, watertight is not tight enough. Working together they have murdered Linnet whilst all the time pretending to hate each other. It is interesting to compare their contrasting attitudes to what they have done. As in Shakespeare's *Macbeth* the responses of murderer and accomplice to the deed are rather different. Jacqueline shows no remorse for the deaths, only sadness for Simon's stupidity. Simon lost his head and admitted everything, even though Poirot had insufficient evidence to convict them. Jacqueline loves Simon with the ferocity of a tigress. One feels Simon is one of those slightly dull, easily swayed, but very handsome young men that Christie often writes about. At the end of the book, a passenger, Mrs Allerton, says that love is frightening, which is why most love stories are tragedies.

Christie often writes about passionate love in a negative way. It is seen as highly destructive of people's ordered lives. In *Sad Cypress* (1940) Mrs Welman says to her niece, Elinor, that caring passionately about someone causes more sorrow than joy, although she adds the commonly expressed thought that those who have never really loved have never really lived. Elinor then bitterly jokes that Mrs Welman sounds like an agony aunt. Mrs Wellman's first name is Laura but Elinor suggests the agony column is Aunt Agatha's. Is this a Freudian slip on the part of Christie? Christie certainly had her own experience of passion. Miss Agatha Miller was engaged to someone else when she met Archie Christie at a dance. Archie, dashing and passionate, insisted she break off her engagement and marry him. In Christie's second book, *The Secret Adversary* (1922), Thomas Beresford and a Miss Prudence Cowley, known as Tuppence, set up the 'Young Adventurers Ltd'. Tommy and Tuppence, like Agatha and Archie Christie, have survived the Great War. They are still young – in their twenties – in love, brimful of energy and with a zest for life. Half a century later, in *Postern of Fate* (1973), Tommy and Tuppence are in their seventies. They retire to the country, still with their faithful servant, Albert. Unlike Marple and Poirot, who start off old and hardly change over the next fifty years, Tommy and Tuppence have aged almost exactly with external time.

When Agatha and Archie Christie's daughter, Rosalind, was only six years old Archie fell in love with a younger woman and demanded a divorce. Agatha Christie was devastated. Like most creative artists, Christie used her pain in her work. In *Sad Cypress* Elinor has lost the man she was engaged to and all Elinor wants to do is to die. Tommy and Tuppence, by contrast, whom Christie created before Archie's affair, remain healthy and faithful to each other forever. Sometimes one can gain comfort by writing, and mentally living, that fictional life.

Christie never wrote about a pair of same-sex lovers as murderers, but she does portray a same-sex couple as sympathetic characters. In England homosexuality was illegal even between consenting adults until 1967 – nearly at the end of Christie's writing career. In a Christie whodunnit it is the puzzle and its solution that are centre stage. Christie usually writes in an unemotional way about death. Most of her victims are either unsympathetic characters or are virtually unknown to the reader. This enables sensitive readers to feel no guilt in enjoying a murder mystery. One of her exceptions is the murder of sweet, kind Amy Murgatroyd in *A Murder Is Announced* (1950) and the grief experienced by her partner, Miss Hinchcliffe. It is almost too painful to read. Christie could write about emotion, as she shows in her novels published under the pen name Mary Westmacott, which are not detective fiction.

In *Evil Under the Sun* (1941), ringing the changes on *Death on the Nile*, the deceiving couple are apparently an unhappy husband and wife, Patrick and Christine Redfern. The Redferns have arguments in front of the other hotel guests. Patrick Redfern openly flirts with another woman, much to the discomfort of all around them. The marriage is clearly over. However, the Redferns are in fact a happily married couple putting on a show to dupe us all. They are out for gain and have been successful in their past criminal actions, which emboldens them. They get a sexual relish from playing this fatal game.

In *Taken at the Flood* (1948) Christie again rings the changes. David Hunter's sister has married a millionaire. The rich couple are killed in the Blitz, but miraculously David and a servant survive the bomb blast. David persuades the servant to pretend to be his sister, so that they can keep their hands on the immense wealth. The money would otherwise revert back to the remaining members of the millionaire's family. Hunter and his sister had arrived in London shortly before the bomb so no one in England had met his sister previously, or so Hunter thinks. Although Hunter and the servant are playing the part of brother and sister, they are in a sexual relationship. The dazzling and charismatic Hunter uses his charm to keep his 'sister' in his thrall. Yet another pairing of lovers, this time pretending to be siblings.

Eight years later, Christie developed a deceptive killer threesome: a mother, her son and his wife. Another pairing is a woman and a gardener, who are actually out for different things, but the route to their goals takes them down a common garden path. In yet another novel there is a housekeeper who cares for an adopted child who grows up to hold sway over her. In most of these pairings the accomplice's motivation is love. The male murderers are more often deceivers, manipulating women through pretended love. But Christie's women too can be deceitful, successfully manipulating those around them. They may use their sexual charms on men, or play the role of a vulnerable female ('I'm all alone and need a friend to confide in') to an unsuspecting woman.

Christie was brought up in an upper-middle-class Victorian household. Her two grandmothers were big influences on her outlook and morality. The morality of divorce is dealt with at more length in the books that Christie published under the pen name, Mary Westmacott, than in her crime novels. But we see perhaps something of her grandmothers in the character of the Victorian matriarch Lady Tressilian, in *Towards Zero*, who accepted in a matter-of-fact way that men had affairs but who did not think that infidelity should break up a marriage.

Christie believed divorce to be wrong. When her first husband, Archie, wanted a divorce, she at first refused. But, in the end, Archie's affair did break up her married life.

CHAPTER EIGHT

Identity theft

People may not be who they seem to be

Plot spoilers for: *Murder in Mesopotamia*; *Dead Man's Folly*.

Identity theft is as ancient as humanity. People have always deceived. In Genesis we read the story of Jacob disguising himself as his older brother Esau in order to get his blind father's blessing and wealth. Jacob's father can distinguish his sons by the amount of hair on their arms. Jacob puts on lambs' skins so that he felt furry to the touch.

After her husband Archie demanded a divorce, Agatha Christie was in utmost despair. She left her home in the night, crashed her car and disappeared. She was apparently in a fugue state. Archie's lover was called Miss Nancy Neele and Agatha booked into a hotel in Harrogate as Mrs Neele. This personal experience of identity theft may have coloured Christie's creative writing.

The alert whodunnit reader will know not to accept any character, however apparently honest or charming, at face value. There are cases of identity theft in about 60% of Christie's novels. In some books virtually everyone is not who they say they are. To muddy the waters a little further some characters have reinvented themselves, for their own personal reasons and unrelated to the central plot. The identity change helps create a red herring. In *Death on the Nile* (1937), for example, there is the wonderful portrayal of Mr Ferguson, an angry young man. Ferguson is typical of many idealists at the University of Oxford who became communist in the 1930s. Ferguson wears torn, dirty shirts and trousers, and enjoys arguing with the other passengers on the Nile steamer. Poirot, however, discovers that under these shabby clothes he wears good quality undergarments. Ferguson turns out to be Lord Dawlish. As a communist Ferguson can't be reconciled with his ancestral privileges but is not quite able to give up the comfy underpants.

Christie based the character, Carlotta Adams, in *Lord Edgware Dies* (1933) on the American actor, Ruth Draper, who gave one-woman shows in London in the 1930s. Draper used one form of identity theft, professional mimicry, to establish her successful career. Watching Ruth Draper perform stimulated Christie's imagination. The plot of *Lord Edgware Dies* hinges on actors and mimics and the identities they can assume.

Identity change, including identity theft, might be for short periods only, for example to establish an alibi. In Christie novels there are jewel thieves pretending to be policeman, and policemen undercover to catch jewel thieves. There are people who change their name for less grand reasons than Lord Dawlish. Perhaps their parents were the victims of a crime and they wish to escape the dark resonances that their surnames will conjure in people's minds. In several Christies there are children, now grown up, who have changed their names to forget their unhappy childhoods. Marriage is not usually thought of as identity theft, but it can be a useful way to hide one's past. Eve Carpenter in *Mrs McGinty's Dead* (1952) earned an unsavoury living during the Second World War being paid for 'dances' with men. Later she marries a wealthy businessman. Now that she has acquired respectability she wishes to keep her past firmly locked away. Carpenter reacts badly to Poirot's investigation, feeling she will be disgraced.

In *Murder in Mesopotamia* (1936) the devastatingly beautiful Louise is married to the head of the archaeological dig, Dr Leidner. Louise had been previously married to a man called Bosner, who had been a German spy. Louise reported Bosner to the authorities, who arrested him. Bosner died in a train crash on the way to prison in 1919. After Bosner's death Louise received threatening letters every time that she became romantically involved. Yet she received no such threats when she met and married Dr Leidner, the kind, sensitive and intelligent archaeologist. The threats restart when Louise falls for Leidner's best friend.

This plot hinges on the combination of a radical identity theft and an unbelievable failure to recognise a former spouse. Bosner, having escaped the train crash, swaps identities with someone who did die in that accident. He studies archaeology, and becomes a respected and loved academic. He has never stopped loving his wife and cannot bear the thought of any other man having a romantic relationship with her. Thirteen years after he dies as Bosner, he remarries Louise as Dr Leidner. He marries his wife twice, without her realising it! Even if he had been disfigured by the train crash, his body odour, his laugh, his mannerisms and his voice would have been instantly recognisable to Louise. Voices do not change until extreme old age. In Dumas' *The Count of Monte Cristo*, the Count is recognised by his lover, Mercedes, although she had been told he had died nine years previously, by the way he twiddled his hair.

Despite this plot weakness *Murder in Mesopotamia* is still a great read. It was for Christie a personal cathartic revenge. Christie had been friends with the exceedingly beautiful Katharine Woolley, married to Sir Leonard Woolley, the Mesopotamian archaeologist. Christie visited their archaeological digs after her divorce, and the Woolleys had stayed at Christie's London house as her guests. Katharine loved having every man in her thrall. She would make the young archaeologists brush her hair or run errands for her. Katharine's previous marriage in 1919 had ended tragically after six months when her husband killed himself. Louise's first marriage, in the novel, also ended in 1919 when Bosner was supposedly killed. It was at the Woolley's dig in Mesopotamia that Christie first met Max Mallowan. They fell in love and married. Katharine Woolley was furious. Katharine refused to allow Christie to stay with Max at the dig in Ur, after their marriage, or even to come to Iraq at all! Christie took revenge by writing about the Woolleys thinly disguised as the Leidners: a different example of identity theft!

With the advantage of time and medical knowledge, we can feel sorry for Katharine Woolley. She was a deeply unhappy person. There are descriptions of Katharine eating kilos of sweets and then making herself vomit, many years before bulimia nervosa was known about or treated. A doctor had examined Katharine, and then spoke to her first husband, who immediately went out and shot himself. It is not known what the doctor found on his examination. Katharine never let Leonard consummate their marriage; she only allowed him to look at her having a bath. Woolley asked his solicitor to file divorce papers, on the grounds of non-consummation. Katharine sadly developed multiple sclerosis, and Woolley felt obliged to look after her until her death. Some have suggested that Katharine Woolley was born with androgen insensitivity syndrome – a condition in which the person is genetically male but looks female. This medical condition was first understood in the 1950s, two decades after *Murder in Mesopotamia* was written.

Dead Man's Folly (1956) is steeped in identity theft. Even the title is a clue: why call the folly *Dead Man's* when Sir George Stubbs, the current owner, is very much alive and built the folly only a year ago? The novel takes place at Nasse House, the ancestral home of the Folliat family. After the death of Mr Folliat and his two sons, the only family survivor was old Mrs Folliat. Mrs Folliat is forced, for tax reasons, to sell the estate to Sir George Stubbs. Early in the book, Poirot commiserates with an ancient retainer saying that it is sad that the days of the Folliats are over. The old man briskly replies that there will always be Folliats at Nasse. If only Poirot had taken this old man seriously, he might have solved the mystery much more quickly than he did.

Sir George Stubbs' wife is a puzzling character. Even Poirot's own observations of her are contradictory. Ariadne Oliver thinks Lady Stubbs beautiful but half-witted. Miss Brewis, Sir George's secretary, believes her to be very shrewd.

Dead Man's Folly has a lot of humour thanks to Ariadne Oliver's personality. Oliver has been commissioned to write a treasure hunt murder mystery for the summer fete. People follow her clues around the garden. The brilliance of Christie's book is that Oliver's treasure hunt is a 'dumb play', just as in Shakespeare's *Hamlet*. In *Hamlet* the players are commanded to perform *The Murder of Gonzago*. They start with a short, mimed summary with a running commentary by Prince Hamlet, so the Court, and especially his uncle, can understand the action. In *Dead Man's Folly* Oliver explains her murder hunt plot to the bewildered Poirot: it seems utterly ludicrous. If you re-read this part *after* you know the solution, you realise it is the dumb play for the book itself. Christie's writing misdirects you into thinking Oliver's mind is hopelessly rambling and eccentric. But the plot is there, laid out for all to read, *before* any of the deaths occur. Mrs Oliver, using her intuition, had realised that all was rotten in this particular English estate.

CHAPTER NINE

Defacing the corpse

Ringing the changes on this whodunnit trope

Plot spoilers for: *The Mystery of the Blue Train.*

On March 5th 1935 Dorothy L Sayers spoke in Oxford on crime fiction. In that lecture she discussed *The Viaduct Murder* (1925) – the first detective novel written by Ronald Knox (he of the Ten Commandments of Detective Fiction – see chapter 1):

> A man is found dead with his face beaten into unrecognizable pulp. Circumstantial evidence suggests that the dead man was X. The detectives and the reader are invited to reason after the following manner:
>
> The man is thought to be X;
>
> But he is unrecognizable;
>
> Therefore he is not X;
>
> Therefore he is some one else, namely Y;
>
> And, since X is undoubtedly missing, X is probably the murderer.
>
> But the disfigured corpse turns out to be X after all; so that all the ingenious conclusions founded upon the false premiss are false also.

'The man is thought to be X; but he is unrecognizable; therefore he is not X'. This simple argument serves us well, and not only in crime novels. Shakespeare used an extreme version of the defaced corpse in *Cymbeline*. Imogen, Cymbeline's daughter, wakes to find, lying next to her, the headless body of a man dressed in her husband's clothes. More familiar, it seems, with her husband's clothes than with his body, she believes the man to be her husband. Shakespeare, however, is no Ronald Knox: the simple argument is all we need. It turns out that Imogen's husband is alive and well and living in Milford Haven.

Christie's first use of the unidentifiable corpse was in her 1925 adventure novel, *The Secret at Chimneys*. The corpse has no more than a walk-on part and, as in Cymbeline, it is misidentified. It is not until *The Mystery of the Blue Train* (1927) that Christie follows Knox in going beyond the simple argument. In that novel the corpse turns out to be exactly who it was thought to have been. The purpose of the defacing, however, was not to hide the identity of the victim. Christie cleverly conceived of a quite different purpose. Someone had impersonated the murdered woman and the corpse was defaced in order to conceal the impersonation.

Christie, as always, continued to work creatively. In a later novel, long before the advent of DNA 'fingerprinting', she had fun in combining identity theft with a defaced corpse to keep the reader guessing. First the corpse appears to be A. Then it is proved to be B. Finally Poirot realises that the 'proof' involved a simple but effective fraud: the corpse was not B after all. It was indeed A. Another variant on the Knox plot.

A few years after that Christie went back to the 'simple argument'. The defaced corpse is not X – the person it is thought to be. But Christie's plot involves *two* corpses and two missing people. One corpse is defaced, the other clearly identified as one of the missing people. So the defaced corpse, it seems, must be the other missing person. Christie simplified that plot in a further novel. The corpse is not defaced but no one can identify it. The reader ponders how to solve a crime when the murder victim is unknown. Poirot suggests, in *Mrs McGinty's Dead* (1952), that if you know the victim well you can identify the murderer – the dead lips, as it were, speak the name.

Christie, and Knox, are not, of course, the only crime writers to make use of unidentified, and unidentifiable, corpses. Indeed Dorothy L Sayers herself uses these plot devices more than once. In her very first whodunnit, *Whose Body?* (1923), a corpse is misidentified although not defaced. In her later novel *The Nine Tailors* (1934) a man's body, mutilated beyond recognition, is found in a woman's grave.

Dorothy L Sayers was three years younger than Christie. Between 1923 and 1937 she published eleven novels starring her aristocratic detective, Lord Peter Wimsey. Time has been less kind to Sayers than to Christie. Before the Second World War Sayers was widely considered the better writer, but her prose has dated in a way that Christie's has not. This is from the first chapter of Sayers' third novel, *Unnatural Death* (1927):

The man with the monocle glanced round the little Soho restaurant with a faint smile. The fat man on the right was unctuously entertaining two ladies of the chorus; beyond him, two elderly habitués were showing their acquaintance with the fare at the 'Au Bon Bourgeois' by consuming a Tripes à la Mode de Caen (which they do very excellently there) and a bottle of Chablis Moutonne 1916; on the other side of the room a provincial and his wife were stupidly clamouring for a cut off the joint with lemonade for the lady and whisky and soda for the gentleman, while at the adjoining table, the handsome silver-haired proprietor, absorbed in fatiguing a salad for a family party, had for the moment no thoughts beyond the nice adjustment of the chopped herbs and garlic. The head waiter, presenting for inspection a plate of Blue River Trout, helped the monocled man and his companion and retired, leaving them in the privacy which unsophisticated people always seek in genteel teashops and never, never find there.

Christie would write eighteen sentences in the space it takes Sayers to write three. A Christie book has more dialogue, shorter sentences and faster pace. Sayers is leisurely, learned and opinionated.

Christie wrote her first novel, *Snow Upon the Desert*, when she was around twenty years old. It was never published but was sent to a family friend, Eden Phillpotts, a successful author who wrote more novels than Christie herself. Phillpotts gave feedback. He praised Christie's feeling for dialogue but advised her not to moralise and not to explain to the reader what her characters really meant. Let the characters speak for themselves, he advised.

Christie took this advice to heart. Unlike many crime writers of the time Christie presents no strong authorial attitude and therefore no attitude that dates. She simply observed, allowing her characters their own foibles, prejudices and voices. Christie dedicated her 1932 novel, *Peril at End House*, to Phillpotts.

For almost thirty years Christie made no use of defaced corpses. Then, in 1971, she published *Nemesis*. This was the last Miss Marple novel that she wrote. The structure of the story is innovative, what might be called a *treasure hunt whodunnit*. From beyond the grave Mr Rafiel challenges Miss Marple to investigate a crime, but he does not tell her what crime. All she is given is a ticket for a coach tour of the famous houses and gardens of Great Britain. We see that at the age of eighty years Christie is still trying out new approaches, and she has lost none of her story-telling technique. But in these final novels one thing is lacking: the plots are no longer cunning. Although the identity of the defaced corpse is central to the solution, there is no twist, no sophistication. The simple argument is all the reader needs. In terms of plot she has returned to *Cymbeline*.

CHAPTER TEN

Time travel

Teasing the reader by distorting time

Plot spoilers for: *The Sittaford Mystery*; *Three Act Tragedy*; *Sleeping Murder*.

A cast-iron alibi: the dream of murderers. Even Poirot admires the writer who can think up a clever ruse. Poirot discusses his magnum opus on detective crime fiction which he is in the process of writing (see *The Clocks*). He praises fictional writer Cyril Quain because of his elaborate alibis. Christie probably had Freeman Wills Crofts in mind as the model for Quain. Crofts was an Irish crime writer. His first novel *The Cask* was published in 1920, the year Poirot was introduced to the world. Crofts wrote over thirty crime novels in the following thirty-seven years. In 1934 he published *The 12.30 from Croydon*, which must have been an inspiration for Christie's 1957 title, *4.50 from Paddington*. Crofts was a railway engineer and his plots often involved the use of train timetables in providing elaborate alibis. Such alibis have fallen out of fashion in crime fiction, perhaps because modern British train timetables represent the triumph of hope over experience.

Christie provided her murderers with alibis in many different ways some of which are discussed in other chapters. The source of poison, for example, might not be what it seems. Sometimes the murder was committed earlier than is assumed. An accomplice, or the murderer, might impersonate the victim after the victim has been killed. In a few novels a device provides misleading evidence for the time of the murder. In one novel an accomplice impersonates the victim and plays dead: the actual murder occurs later than is thought. Occasionally the alibi is provided by an accomplice impersonating the murderer. In one novel that accomplice is an innocent dupe.

One of the most enjoyable ways in which Christie provides the murderer with an alibi is through using time travel to distort time. She does this in two different ways. The first involves the murderer travelling much faster than seems possible. The second is through deceiving readers about the relative timing of different events. Sometimes she combines the two.

The Sittaford Mystery (1931) provides an example of the first method. Major Burnaby is, rather reluctantly, attending a séance. Immediately after the séance he sets off through deep snow to visit his friend, Captain Trevelyan, who lives six miles away. He arrives at his friend's house to find him dead – murdered a couple of hours previously and at around the time of the séance. Christie's description of Burnaby's arrival at the house of his murdered friend is masterly. In just one sentence Christie conjures up in our imagination a vivid picture of the hunched figure of Major Burnaby making his way slowly through the driving snow. We are unlikely to imagine that same Burnaby skiing rapidly and confidently over the snow two hours earlier to commit the murder. Christie's ability to create a vivid scene is one of the reasons why her novels transfer so well to TV and film. She also puts it to good use to deceive readers, as this example illustrates.

In *Three Act Tragedy* (1934) she again makes use of her literary skills to paint a picture that obfuscates the truth. The novel is divided into three 'acts'. At the end of Act One we learn that Sir Charles Cartwright has gone to the South of France. At the beginning of Act Two we learn that Mr Satterthwaite a few days later also travelled to the French Riviera. As Mr Satterthwaite is sitting out in the sun he reads the report in a two-day-old English newspaper of the death of Sir Bartholomew Strange. At that moment he sees Sir Charles Cartwright dressed smartly in yachting costume. Cartwright comes up to Satterthwaite and asks whether he has heard that Strange has died. He goes on to suggest that Strange's death might not have been due to natural causes and that it has similarities with a murder that both Cartwright and Satterthwaite had previously witnessed.

At no point does Christie lie to the reader. Most of us will be imagining Sir Charles well settled into his life in the South of France. We will simply assume that he has been there ever since he left England, at which time Sir Bartholomew Strange was alive and well. Christie deceives through a combination of the careful placing of information together with her deft use of description and dialogue.

Sleeping Murder (1976) provides another good example of Christie's skill at deceiving us about the timing of events. In this novel she deceives by breaking with literary convention. Several of the chapters are divided into numbered sections. In the first section of one of the chapters three people are waiting for the arrival of Lily Kimble. In the second section we are with Lily Kimble as she is murdered, many miles from the location in the first section. In the third section we are back with the three people waiting for Lily Kimble to arrive, which she never does. It is as though each of the three people has a perfect alibi. In the fourth section the three people have gone to the local police station, where Inspector Last tells them that Lily Kimble has been murdered. There follows a detailed discussion of train timetables from which we *could* work out that Lily Kimble had been murdered several hours before the three people met up. The events described in the second section of the chapter – including Lily Kimble's murder – in fact took place some hours before the events described in the first and third sections. Such time shifts – back and then forward – in the same chapter and without clear signposting, is unconventional. Most readers will unconsciously make the conventional assumption: that Lily Kimble was murdered whilst the three people were together, waiting. The mental image of these events taking place at the same time makes a stronger impression than the rather dull discussion of railway timetables.

Sleeping Murder was the last of Christie's novels to be published – in October 1976, nine months after Christie had died. It was written as Miss Marple's final case. A year earlier Poirot's last case *Curtain* had been published. Both novels had been written several decades previously and kept in aspic until it was clear that Christie would write no more books.

In October 1940 Christie's London house, in Sheffield Terrace, Kensington, had narrowly escaped when a bomb flattened most of the street during the Blitz. Christie, it has been widely thought, feeling the need to ensure a nest egg for her family in case she was killed, wrote both novels shortly afterwards. The potential royalties for *Sleeping Murder* were given to Christie's husband, Max, and those for *Curtain* to her daughter, Rosalind.

Christie, however, has, perhaps unwittingly, deceived us about the timing of the writing of *Sleeping Murder*. It was almost certainly written well after the Second World War. By 1940 Christie had published only one novel and two collections of short stories featuring Miss Marple. In contrast she had already published twenty Poirot novels. Tommy and Tuppence were more established than Miss Marple at this stage. In *Sleeping Murder* Colonel Melrose clearly refers to one of Miss Marple's earlier cases, which is the subject of *The Moving Finger*, published in 1942. Gwenda, the central character in *Sleeping Murder*, goes to the 'Witmore Theatre' (a made-up name) in London to see the actor John Gielgud in *The Duchess of Malfi*. When Gwenda leaves the theatre she walked rapidly along the Haymarket. In fact John Gielgud did star in *The Duchess of Malfi* at the Theatre Royal in the Haymarket for a season in 1944–45. It seems highly likely that Christie saw this production and that it was the inspiration for the novel's dramatic early scene, and the lurking incest.

John Curran, in his meticulous study of Christie's notebooks, has shed further light on the timing of *Sleeping Murder*. In a notebook entry dated 1948 Christie outlines plot ideas that must relate to what became *Sleeping Murder*. So at this point the book was still in the planning stages. Curran believes that the novel was not written until late 1948 or 1949. But even this may be too early. By the end of 1949 only three Miss Marple novels had been published. By 1953, however, there were a further three. Marple was by then Christie's most important detective after Poirot and, at last, deserving of a final case.

John Curran's researching amongst Christie's notebooks also reveal the vicissitudes in the making and naming of *Sleeping Murder*. Christie hesitated as to which detective to include and indeed Marple feels something of an afterthought. The central characters are Gwenda and Giles Reed, a recently married couple, she lively and intelligent, he a little dull. Sound familiar? Very like the young Tommy and Tuppence. The title changed several times during the slow incubation. The traces of this history can be seen in some of the chapter titles, rather as English place names sustain a lingering memory of long-lost features of a village. The title to one chapter, *Murder in Retrospect*, was an early possibility but had to be abandoned when it was used by the American publishers for her novel *Five Little Pigs* (1942). *Cover Her*

Face, from a line in Webster's *The Duchess of Malfi*, had to be abandoned when P.D. James used the title in 1962. It remains as the title to chapter 3. The final title is from a line spoken by Miss Marple's doctor, Dr Haydock – a variation on *let sleeping dogs lie*.

Is *Sleeping Murder* Miss Marple's final case? There is just one hint near the end that she may be seriously ill. Gwenda suggests that Miss Marple does not look well and begins to ask whether there is anything wrong, but Miss Marple brushes the question aside and rapidly changes the subject. Perhaps Gwenda's concern is misplaced. Perhaps if we were able to travel in time we would find that Miss Marple had successfully solved further crimes; and, perhaps, if time could be sufficiently distorted, Christie might be persuaded to tell us about them.

CHAPTER ELEVEN

The locked room

Variations on a classic theme

Plot spoilers for: *They Do It with Mirrors*.

Towards the end of his career Hercule Poirot is writing a book on crime fiction (see *The Clocks*). He doesn't mention Conan Doyle's *The Adventure of the Speckled Band* (1892) and contemptuously dismisses Poe's *The Mystery in the Rue Morgue* (1841): two famous locked-room mysteries. He is, however, greatly admiring of Gaston Leroux's 1907 novel *The Mystery of the Yellow Room*. Leroux is now better remembered for another work, *The Phantom of the Opera* – the basis for one of the most successful musicals of all time.

Christie may never have written whodunnits had it not been for Leroux's locked-room mystery – and a bit of sibling rivalry. Christie's sister, Madge, was eleven years older than Agatha. She had had several short stories published. Agatha admired her sister but was also perhaps a little envious of her success. After they had both enjoyed *The Mystery of the Yellow Room* Madge challenged Agatha to write a murder mystery of her own. Christie's response was *The Mysterious Affair at Styles*, her first published novel and the first to feature Hercule Poirot. There is a lot of Conan Doyle in that first novel. In Conan Doyle the clues are, in the main, to show the brilliance of Sherlock Holmes. In *The Mystery of the Yellow Room* there are clues which the reader can use to solve the plot. The plot has two separate puzzles: how was the crime committed, and how, on a later occasion, did the villain apparently vanish into thin air? In *The Mysterious Affair at Styles* most of the clues show the brilliance of Poirot. As Christie matured the influence of Conan Doyle waned, and the influence of Leroux waxed.

The locked-room mystery might be seen as a type of whodunnit in which the central mystery is less *who* did it, and more *how* did they do it? Its essence is that a crime (usually murder) is found to have been committed in a room (or other limited space) from which no one could have escaped without detection. The criminal is not in the room and was not seen escaping from it. Christie's first novel was *not* a locked-room mystery, but in later books she explored and played with the theme, and, being Christie, she invented new twists.

In *The Mystery of the Yellow Room* a professor hears sounds of a terrible struggle, furniture crashing to the floor and his daughter screaming, all from the adjacent locked bedroom. When he eventually breaks down the door he finds his half-strangled daughter, alone. No one is hiding under the bed, or in the wardrobe. The window shutters are tightly bolted from the inside.

Christie echoes this scene in *Hercule Poirot's Christmas* (1938). The murder is highly theatrical with loud crashing sounds of falling furniture, and an eerie scream. Simeon Lee is found dead behind a locked door, with the key on the inside and no possible exit for the murderer. Tables and chairs are strewn around the room, and there is a lot of blood. Christie seems to be re-writing Leroux, but almost immediately the locked door is explained: thin-nosed pliers were used to turn the barrel of the key through the keyhole from the outside. Christie has turned the question from *how* did the villain do it, to *why* did he bother to lock the door at all? As Poirot points out, locking the door only wastes valuable time. Poirot reasons that if the murderer had locked the door from the outside just after the sound of the crashing furniture and the scream he would have been caught red-handed. This is the critical clue. As in Leroux's *Yellow Room*, timing is the key that unlocks the door and the mystery.

Murder in Mesopotamia (1936) is Christie's 'straight' locked-room mystery, or rather a *watched*-room mystery. This novel is set on an archaeological dig in the Middle East. The expedition house is square with a single, central space – a courtyard that can be entered only through a single archway. The individual rooms can be accessed only through doors opening into this central space. The beautiful Louise Leidner is found, murdered, alone in her bedroom. No one could have entered the courtyard without being seen by an Arab boy who was washing pots. Over the critical period when the murder happened no one was seen entering or exiting either the courtyard or

Louise Leidner's room. The small windows on the external walls of each room are barred. Poirot sticks his head out through the bars of the window of Leidner's room but cannot get his shoulders through, so satisfying himself that no one could have got in or out that way. Examination of the room shows a bloodstain on the carpet by the washstand. Perhaps the killer washed the blood away, carelessly dripping some on the carpet. The solution is fair and well clued but not obvious.

In Poirot's last case, *Curtain*, there is *the perfect* locked-room murder, although it is not the central puzzle, and never really a puzzle at all. It is as though Christie wanted Poirot to make a final tribute to Leroux. The murder is so perfect that it remains unsolved even at the time of Poirot's death. In fact there is nothing to solve because although someone *has* been murdered, the coroner's verdict is suicide, and the police are never involved. But of course Poirot has to have the last word, even from beyond the grave. Four months after Poirot's death from a heart attack, Hastings receives a letter. It is the last big reveal – a letter from Poirot explaining what had really happened.

Christie's most innovative take on the locked-room mystery is a *locked-out*-room mystery. The theme of *They Do It with Mirrors* (1952) is that nothing is as it seems. The world is turned on its head, or more accurately, becomes a mirror's reflection. The book is set in a boys' borstal. The philanthropic owners have converted their country house and provide all the money to run it. In one scene the head of the institution and a young man are having a terrible row in the head's locked study. The lights go out – a blown fuse. The house is in darkness. Everyone else is huddled around the outside of the study door as the row continues inside. A gun goes off inside the study. Fortunately it turns out that the two people inside the study are unharmed – the bullet hit the woodwork. During this rumpus, someone entirely different is murdered in another room in a distant part of the mansion. The head and the young man have the perfect alibi since by being locked *in* the study they are locked *out* of the possibility of being suspects.

The murder scene in *Death in the Clouds* (1935) is inspired by the idea of a locked room although the novel is not a locked-room mystery. The locked room in question is the first-class passenger compartment of a small aircraft. There are eleven passengers alive at the start of the flight from Paris, but only ten alive when the plane lands in Croydon. The locked room is jam-packed with people. The mystery is not how did the murderer escape the room but how was it possible that no one noticed the murder? Even the great Hercule Poirot, who was one of the passengers, saw and heard nothing. Poirot's excuse was that he was travel-sick!

One of Christie's masterpieces, *And Then There Were None* (1939), is a locked-room mystery that isn't a locked-room mystery. The murders take place on an island. At the end of the novel the authorities find a number of corpses, all apparently the victims of murder, but no murderer. No one could have left the island without being detected. In this novel, however, Christie is using the structure of a locked-room mystery to write a completely different kind of crime novel. The focus of the mystery is not how the murderer escapes the island but the much more general question: what on earth is going on?

CLUES

CHAPTER TWELVE

Beyond the deerstalker

Throwing away the hat and magnifying glass

No plot spoilers.

Plots and misdirections aim to deceive. It is the clues that help the reader solve the puzzle. Christie began by imitating Conan Doyle. Most of the clues in her first whodunnit show perhaps the brilliance of Poirot but they are of little use to the reader. Within only a few years, however, Christie had developed a quite different approach: clues that help the reader find the solution. And what an astonishing variety of types of clue she created!

Sherlock Holmes was introduced to the world in 1887 in Conan Doyle's novel *A Study in Scarlet.* This is how Dr Watson describes Holmes examining the crime scene in their first case together:

> As he spoke, he whipped a tape measure and a large round magnifying glass from his pocket. With these two implements he trotted noiselessly about the room, sometimes stopping, occasionally kneeling and once

> lying flat upon his face … As I watched him I was
> irresistibly reminded of a pure-blooded, well-trained
> foxhound as it dashes backwards and forwards through
> the covert, whining in its eagerness, until it comes
> across the lost scent.

Holmes carefully measures the distance between marks that are invisible to Watson, and gathers up a pile of grey dust from the floor, packing it away in an envelope.

We first meet Hercule Poirot in Christie's novel *The Mysterious Affair at Styles*, published in 1920. At the crime scene Poirot could be Holmes. He carefully inspects the room, rapidly flitting from one object to another. He carries with him a pair of forceps which he uses to pull out a tiny particle from the bolt of a door and then places the particle carefully in an envelope. He smells an almost invisible stain on the carpet. He dusts a fragment of charred paper for fingerprints and transfers a few drops of coffee into test tubes.

Poirot, in this first novel, is already complete with those mannerisms and foibles that seem to define him. We learn of his little grey cells and his obsessional straightening of ornaments. He builds houses from playing cards, and gathers the suspects for the denouement. We are told of his egg-shaped head and the way that his eyes turn green, like a cat's, when he is excited. In the most important aspect of his character, however, that is in his behaviour as a detective, this early Poirot is quite different from what he will become. In the first novel, Poirot is simply a Belgian Sherlock Holmes. His focus is on what might be called *sleuth clues* – physical clues requiring careful, often minute observation. These clues do not help the reader solve the mystery. There *are* clues that help the reader in this first Poirot novel, but they are fewer than the sleuth clues, and, by Christie's later standards, somewhat desultory.

In the second Poirot novel, *The Murder on the Links* (1923), we see Christie in the process of undergoing the major transformation in her development as a whodunnit writer. It is a novel in transit. Christie is no longer the caterpillar that she was in *The Mysterious Affair at Styles* but not yet the butterfly that she will become. This new approach requires a metamorphosis in Poirot. In *The Murder on the Links* the transformation is not complete and the result is a Poirot of contrasts and conflicts.

Hastings, the narrator, alerts us early on to the new Poirot. He tells us that Poirot disdains such evidence – such sleuth clues as footprints and cigarette ash, but immediately there is a qualification. Poirot's view is that such evidence *taken by itself* would never enable a detective to solve a problem. The sleuth clues are still significant. But how significant? In order to contrast the methods of Poirot with those that focus on sleuth clues Christie creates the character of Giraud, a senior detective from Paris. Giraud examines in great detail the scenes of the crimes. At one point he discovers a cigarette end and a match. He complacently tells Poirot that the match is common in South America. Poirot, echoing Watson, contemptuously refers to Giraud as the human foxhound.

Poirot, however, in this novel is still something of a foxhound himself. He finds a torn cheque under a rug, a strand of hair on the back of a chair; he makes deductions from the absence of dust, and carefully examines the second corpse. None of this is helpful to the reader in solving the puzzle.

In *The Murder on the Links* there are two crimes: the main crime that is the focus at the denouement and a subsidiary crime that is solved halfway through the novel. The clues to the main crime are poor and the solution arbitrary. The clues to the subsidiary crime, however, are an intimation of what Christie will go on to achieve. Readers who hit on the solution to the subsidiary crime will feel confident that they are correct. The crucial point is that these clues are not *sleuth* clues; they are instead about how the characters behave and what they say.

In parallel with how Christie is developing the clues, Poirot is changing how he thinks. In *The Mysterious Affair at Styles* Poirot explains his approach to detection in terms of following the links of a chain: one fact leading to another. Of particular significance is the little detail that does not quite fit.

In *The Murder on the Links* Poirot again explains his methods, but they no longer involve forging a chain from small details. What Poirot emphasises is *psychology*. What interests him at this point in the novel is not sleuth clues but the ways in which one of the characters shows a change in behaviour.

Whereas readers can only watch from the sidelines as Holmes or Poirot solve the crime from sleuth clues, they can join Poirot in a race to the solution when it is the psychological points that are crucial.

In *The Murder on the Links* Poirot is beginning to distance himself from Sherlock Holmes, and Christie is developing clues that can engage the reader in solving the puzzle, but Conan Doyle still lurks in the background. There is a wonderfully Holmesian moment when Poirot is told of the discovery of the second body. At first he is mortified – he had not predicted a second murder. But then he relaxes and accurately describes the second body, although he has not seen it. Hastings and the reader are impressed. Twelve years and fifteen novels later (in *The A.B.C. Murders*, 1936), by which time Christie has fully developed her mature style, she mocks this kind of deduction. Poirot and Hastings are seated in a first-class railway carriage (a setting straight out of Conan Doyle). Hastings is eager to learn what Poirot has deduced from their visit to the scene of the first murder. Poirot describes the appearance of the murderer in minute detail. For a moment Hastings is taken in. Poirot chastises him and says that he is not Sherlock Holmes and that he knows nothing about the murderer.

The first two Poirot novels are part whodunnit and part Sherlock Holmes. It is not until *The Murder of Roger Ackroyd* (1926), her sixth published novel and the third starring Hercule Poirot, that Christie writes a pure whodunnit. It is in this novel that Christie becomes the butterfly, emerging from the shadow of Conan Doyle – the novel in which Poirot throws away the metaphorical magnifying glass and deerstalker.

The deerstalker hat, by the way, is never explicitly mentioned in the Conan Doyle stories. We owe the origin of that definitive image of Holmes in Inverness cape and deerstalker to Sidney Paget's illustrations in *The Strand Magazine* that accompanied Conan Doyle's *The Boscombe Valley Mystery* (1891). There is, however, mention, in a later story, *The Adventure of Silver Blaze* (1892), of Holmes wearing an 'ear-flapped travelling cap', which could refer to a deerstalker – an example perhaps of literature following art. It is in *Silver Blaze* that Colonel Ross says to Holmes: 'Is there any other point to which you would wish to draw my attention?' which leads to the immortal lines:

> 'To the curious incident of the dog in the night-time.'
> 'The dog did nothing in the night-time.'
> 'That is the curious incident,' remarked Sherlock Holmes.

CHAPTER THIRTEEN

The dog that didn't bark

Nothing *is* the clue

Plot spoilers for: *Towards Zero.*

Positive clues leap out of the text. The challenge to the reader in most whodunnits is to understand the significance of a scrap of clothing caught on a nail, the footprints under a windowsill or fingerprints smeared on a beer bottle. An *absence* of something is much harder to spot. Our brains have evolved to be alert to a positive change in sound, light, smell or touch. It is much more difficult to say when a pain ceased than when it started. Such focus on positive change has enormous survival advantage when the slightest rustle in a bush could be a sabre-toothed tiger. A negative clue, nothing but silence, will pass us by, unnoticed in the text.

Sherlock Holmes' 'curious incident of the dog in the night-time' has become the most famous negative clue in crime literature in part due to Mark Haddon's brilliant best-seller. Sherlock Holmes was making a point about the silent dog in the story. It did *not* bark when a horse was stolen, leading Holmes to deduce that the dog must have known and trusted the thief. Our own family dog was quite the reverse, excitedly barking by the front door to welcome our children home but completely ignoring strangers, even when they walked into our kitchen at 3am. Clearly our dog was not a Conan Doyle fan, unlike Agatha Christie, who knew his works well. There is a clear tribute to Holmes in Christie's third novel, *The Murder on the Links* (1923). Poirot draws attention to the issue of footprints. M Giraud, the French police inspector and butt of many of Poirot's jibes, says that he cannot see any footprints. Poirot smugly replies that there aren't any.

Poirot later explains patiently to Hastings that there should have been footprints because the gardener had just planted out the flowerbeds. Someone must have escaped by the window, jumped down onto the soft soil and then raked over the flowerbed to obliterate their footprints. By doing so, they inadvertently smoothed over the gardener's boot marks as well.

Poirot is a Conan Doyle fan, too, albeit a critical one. In his magnum opus on detective fiction (see *The Clocks*) Poirot describes Conan Doyle as the *Maître*, although this is for the pleasure of the language and the art of the writing, rather than for the plots, which Poirot thinks are far-fetched. Towards the end of *The Clocks* Poirot describes an absence of a feature of a crime, a feature that should be present, as a Sherlock Holmes crime. The very crime that Poirot is investigating is in fact a Sherlock Holmes crime. One of the key clues is an absence – a metaphorical dog that didn't bark. In *The Clocks* Christie is generously giving us a positive clue about a negative clue.

Fingerprints, or rather the lack of them, provides an important clue in *Five Little Pigs* (1942) when Amyas is poisoned by hemlock in his beer. There are no fingerprints on the beer bottle. But Christie, as so often, rings the changes. The absence of fingerprints does not prove that someone is guilty: rather it proves that one of the suspects is innocent.

In *The A.B.C. Murders* (1936), Christie again plays with the absence of fingerprints. This time it is not a clue but a gentle dig at Hastings, and, again, a homage to Conan Doyle. When a copy of the ABC Railway Guide is found at the scene of the murder Hastings asks Poirot whether he thinks that the murderer left it by mistake. Poirot says that the murderer left it on purpose – it is the fingerprints that tell us that. Hastings, as usual, falls into Poirot's trap and points out that there were no fingerprints. Precisely. The murderer must have carefully wiped the railway guide clean.

In *Death in the Clouds* (1935), written just the year before *The A.B.C. Murders*, Poirot uses fingerprints that don't exist to trick a murderer into confessing. At the big reveal Poirot knows who the murderer is, but he needs more evidence. He tells the murderer that his fingerprints were on the bottle. The murderer, like Hastings, falls for Poirot's trap and begins to say that that cannot be true since he wore gloves.

Professor Earl F Bargainnier, in his excellent book *The Gentle Art of Murder*, points out another more subtle example of a dog that didn't bark in *Towards Zero* (1944). When we read the novel this particular clue completely passed us, silently, by. *Towards Zero* is a cleverly constructed book. It has a slow first half with no apparent murders and many separate story lines that seem irrelevant. At a dinner party, an old lawyer, Treves, is wittering on about a case he was involved in in which a child died. At the end of the book you realise that Treves was issuing a direct warning to the murderer. By the next morning Treves, of course, is dead. The clue we missed was that everyone at the party was excitedly cross-questioning Treves for more details about the case he had spoken about. Every person, that is, except one who remains silent throughout: the dog that didn't bark out a question.

Christie also wrote about real dogs as characters, although they all bark. Indeed, in *Towards Zero* there is a wire-haired terrier, Don, of amiable and loving disposition who noses out a very critical clue, barking with excitement. Bob is another Christie fictional wire-haired terrier. He is the *Dumb Witness* (1937) of that novel's title. We get to know his thoughts. Hastings bonds with Bob and they happily scamper off into the sunset together at the end of the book.

Christie also dedicated books to her dogs. Peter, her own beloved wire-haired terrier, had just died when she wrote *Dumb Witness*. The love Christie had for her dog, and that comes through in the writing, is very moving. Peter was Christie's faithful companion and loving friend through the double heartbreak of her mother's death and her (first) husband, Archie, leaving their family home for a younger woman. As Christie wrote to her second husband, Max Mallowan, in 1930, Peter was all she had had to hold on to through those difficult times. The museum in Wallingford in Oxfordshire, where Christie had a home, provides information that in fact it was another of Christie's dogs, Binkie, who, like Bob in *Dumb Witness*, left toys on the stairs as a trip hazard.

Postern of Fate (1973) is dedicated to her final dog, Hannibal, a Manchester terrier that nipped most people, and his master – Sir Max Mallowan, Christie's second husband. Indeed, Hannibal's fictional portrayal has him leaping like a Bengal tiger in defence of Tuppence, saving her life. Hannibal's fault in real life is turned into a fictional asset.

Christie not only put dogs in many of her books but uses dog and cat metaphors to describe humans. Poirot is often described as having eyes glowing green like a cat's when he is about to pounce on the murderer. The excitement of the big reveal, the thrill of the hunt, knowing success is within his grasp. Poirot shows the reader his feline side. Cats, however, as a description are usually reserved for rather cruel, self-centred women, although there are exceptions. In *Murder in Mesopotamia* (1936), Dr Reilly describes the dazzlingly beautiful Louise Leidner as a cat, who enjoys playing with people as cats play with mice, and observing their suffering.

Humans who are likened to dogs, however, are almost always fundamentally good, in a Christie novel. Time and again Poirot turns to Hastings, just as Christie relied on her dog, Peter, in times of doubt or stress. Both are relationships of pure friendship and mutual trust. Poirot describes Hastings as of the bulldog breed (*Lord Edgware Dies*, 1933) and as the faithful dog who will protect him (*Curtain*, 1975). Christie does not confine her dog metaphors to Captain Hastings. Whenever Christie uses a canine simile or metaphor we know that the author has a respect and warmth for that character. Bundle, the feisty heroine in *Chimneys* (1925), describes Mr Eversleigh as a faithful dog. This tells us that Bill Eversleigh will turn out to be loyal, brave, lovable and trustworthy but not necessarily the brightest or shrewdest of men.

In *Death in the Clouds* (1935), Lord Horbury has become completely disillusioned about his beautiful, young wife whom he sees as vulgar and vicious. By contrast he loves his spaniel, Betsy, and wonders why the word bitch is a term of disparagement. Betsy, he thinks, is worth more than almost all the women, put together, he has ever met.

CHAPTER FOURTEEN

Deduction

Thinking through the implications of a single clue

Plot spoilers for: *The Sittaford Mystery.*

One of Christie's greatest skills as a setter of puzzles was to provide many clues, none of which by itself is sufficient, but taken together they provide powerful evidence for the solution (see chapter 19). She does this again and again. Just occasionally she gives a clue that is sufficient by itself, but only if the reader thinks carefully through all the implications. Applying the term rather loosely we call this process of thinking through the implications of a single clue, *deduction.* Logicians will wince. Although we are misusing the term, however, we follow no less an authority than Sherlock Holmes himself.

According to Holmes there are three qualities necessary for the ideal detective: the power of observation, the power of deduction and knowledge. Watson says (*The Sign of Four*):

'But you spoke just now of observation and deduction. Surely the one to some extent implies the other.'

'Why, hardly,' [Holmes] answered, leaning back luxuriously in his armchair and sending up thick blue wreaths from his pipe. 'For example, observation shows me that you have been to the Wigmore Street Post Office this morning, but deduction lets me know that when there you dispatched a telegram.'

Holmes talks often about the 'science of deduction'. Deduction, for logicians, is a precise form of argument. It is the process of deriving a logically valid conclusion from premisses. The classical form of deductive argument is the syllogism. For example:

Premiss 1: All those who have died in a crime novel have been murdered;
Premiss 2: Mrs Smith, a character in a crime novel, has died (apparently from suicide);
Conclusion: Mrs Smith has been murdered.

The conclusion will be true if both (all) premisses are true *and* if the conclusion follows logically from the premisses. In the above syllogism the conclusion does follow logically from the premisses but *Premiss 1* is false. Perhaps most dead bodies in a crime novel have died as a result of murder but not all. The conclusion, therefore, is not necessarily true. Christie, and other whodunnit writers, occasionally trick readers whose natural assumption is to believe *Premiss 1*. Indeed, in one Christie story a death which looks like a murder turns out to have been suicide (chapter 5).

So what form of reasoning does Holmes use when he 'deduces' that Watson sent a telegram? Holmes' reasoning goes like this. Holmes and Watson were in the same room before Watson went to the post office. Holmes therefore knew that Watson had not written a letter that morning. Furthermore, Holmes could see that Watson already had plenty of stamps and postcards on his desk. The only reason left for going to the post office was to send a telegram. 'Eliminate all other factors, and the one which remains must be the truth,' says Holmes. Elementary, my dear Watson!

We could, just about, twist Holmes' reasoning into a kind of deduction. We would need to *assume* some premisses as follows:

Premiss 1: There are only four reasons to go into a post office: to post a letter, to buy stamps, to buy postcards and to send a telegram.

Premiss 2: Watson went into a post office.

Premiss 3: Watson had no letter to post and no reason to buy stamps or postcards.

Premiss 4: Watson would not go into a post office if he had no reason to do so.

Conclusion: Watson went into the post office to send a telegram.

Deduction starts from established facts and generalisations (the premisses) and aims to find what follows logically from those premises. One way of thinking of deduction is that it clarifies what is already implicit in the premises. It introduces no new idea but simply makes visible what is already there.

Sherlock Holmes did not start with generalisations but with a specific observation (that Watson had visited the post office). He then thought about what reasons Watson might have for visiting the post office – to post a letter, for example. He sought further evidence relevant to these reasons – evidence that might support or rebut them. In light of all the evidence Holmes then decided on the most likely *hypothesis* that could account for the original observation. This process of reasoning, unlike valid deduction, is not logically watertight. Other hypotheses could account for Watson's visit to the post office. For example, he may have written a letter the night before, or he was perhaps buying stamps for a friend.

Logicians call Holmes' reasoning *abduction*. It is how doctors make a diagnosis. A doctor, if the job is being done properly, asks the patient about the symptoms and their history. She then carries out a relevant physical examination looking for signs of illness. She then forms a 'differential diagnosis' – hypotheses about what could account for the signs and symptoms. The doctor might order a number of investigations, such as blood tests. Based on the signs, symptoms and test results the doctor, just like Holmes, *abducts* the best hypothesis to account for the results. That is she comes to a (provisional) diagnosis.

What kind of reasoning does Agatha Christie demand from us when she provides a 'deductive' clue? A good example is in *The Sittaford Mystery* (1931). The most brilliant scene in that novel is early on when six people gather for a séance. They sit round a table in the dark. The table begins to rock. Contact is made with a spirit. The spirit has a message for Major Burnaby, one of the six people. The message, spelt out letter by letter, says that Trevelyan has been murdered. And indeed it turns out that Captain Trevelyan has been murdered, six miles away, and close to the time that the séance was taking place. This is good drama, which helps hide the fact that it is also a subtle but major clue. The reader can identify the murderer with a high degree of confidence directly from the séance, but there are seven steps. The reasoning is as follows:

1. The message cannot be from the spirit world – not in an Agatha Christie novel.
2. A coherent, and correct, message could only be formed if one of the six people around the table made it happen.
3. The person who manipulated the table must have known that the message would turn out to be true.
4. Why would someone want to announce the murder? The best way of seeking the reason is to examine the effect.
5. The only effect of the announcement is that it gives Major Burnaby a reason to visit Trevelyan straight away.
6. If anyone other than Major Burnaby were the murderer there would have been no reason to announce Trevelyan's murder.

7. Therefore, since the murder was announced, Burnaby must be the murderer.

A reader who thinks carefully about the séance and its effects will be almost certain to reach this conclusion, and will then focus on discovering the mechanism.

The reasoning outlined above is not watertight. Indeed later in the book Christie, aware that readers might wonder about the séance, provides an alternative hypothesis as distraction (chapter 28). If thought through carefully, however, by far the most likely hypothesis to account for the facts of the séance is that Burnaby is the murderer. Sherlock Holmes would have got there rather more quickly than the feisty, but rather unpleasant, sleuth Emily Trefusis. Strictly speaking this is another example of abduction. The step-by-step reasoning, however, justifies calling it *deduction*, using the term in its everyday, informal attire.

In some books Christie gives us a clue with two faces, a double clue that combines deduction with analogy. First we must realise that what looks unconnected provides in fact an analogy to the principal crime. Then we must make use of our little grey cells. Rather than seeing in a flash what the analogy is we have to work it out, step by step.

CHAPTER FIFTEEN

Clues by analogy

A scene unrelated to the murder resonates with the solution

Plot spoilers for: *Evil Under the Sun*; *Sparkling Cyanide*.

Our favourite of all Christie's clues are her clues by analogy. They are elegant, clever, satisfying and rare. They require us to see something in common between the clue and the solution. 'A correspondence in certain respects between things otherwise different' is how one dictionary defines *analogy*.

Christie uses analogies in two different ways. One way requires us to work through the analogy using 'deductive' thinking (chapter 14). The other needs us to see the point with a flash of insight. A good example of the first is in *Evil Under the Sun* (1941). The novel is set on an island off the English coast. Patrick Redfern, a good-looking young married man, has been flirting with actress, Arlena Marshall. One morning, somewhat surprisingly, Patrick asks the athletic Emily Brewster if he can join her in her rowing boat. They set off to row round the island. As they come to Pixy Cove they see a woman lying on the beach. They land the boat. Patrick rushes up to her. She does not move. Patrick tells Emily that she is dead. When the corpse – that of Arlena Marshall – is examined by the authorities some hours later it is clear that she was strangled. Poirot asks the police to find out about other recent cases of strangulation.

One such case was the murder of Alice Corrigan. Poirot believes that the same person killed Alice Corrigan and Arlena Marshall. We are given a synoptic summary of the case of Alice Corrigan and Poirot makes it clear that there is an analogy between the murder of Alice Corrigan and that of Arlena Marshall. Knowing this the reader can reason as follows. Either the husband or the hiker must have killed Alice Corrigan as there is no one else in the story. The hiker who found the dead body and reported it sometime later to the police was not suspected. She was a reliable school games mistress, she had no motive and the killer almost certainly had large hands. The husband must, therefore, have been the killer and so his alibi must be false. The only way that that could be true is if the hiker had lied, and the actual time of the murder was later than had been assumed. How does all this relate to the murder of Arlena? At first it does not seem to fit. Arlena's dead body was seen by two people: Patrick Redfern and Emily Brewster. What is similar, however, is that Arlena's body was not examined by the authorities until sometime later. Almost everyone has an alibi for the time up to and including when Patrick and Emily discovered the body. But suppose, as in the Corrigan case, Arlena was actually murdered *after* the discovery of the body. In that case Patrick and Emily might be in it together, but then whose body was it on the beach? Alternatively the person on the beach was Patrick's accomplice, pretending to be the dead body of Arlena so as to fool Emily.

Not all of Christie's analogy clues need to be thought through in this way. Some can inspire that eureka moment, as in *Sparkling Cyanide* (1945). A year before the novel opens Rosemary Barton died from cyanide poison while dining at a posh London restaurant, The Luxembourg. It was assumed that she had committed suicide. Rosemary's husband, George, becomes suspicious that his wife had been murdered by one of the people at the dinner. He decides to repeat the dinner – the same restaurant and the same diners. He is hoping to shock the murderer into making a confession. The central scene in the novel is this repeat dinner. Partway through the evening the diners leave the table to dance. Just before they get up they toast Rosemary's younger sister, Iris, who is one of the diners. It is her birthday. After the dancing the diners return to the table. Mr Barton toasts the memory of Rosemary: he picks up his glass, drinks and dies. The obvious motive for Barton's murder is that he was about to unmask the person who had murdered Rosemary.

There is a curious tiny incident that readers who know Christie will realise must be important. During the dancing a waiter approaches the empty table, which is round. He picks up a handbag which had dropped to the floor and puts it back on the table. At first this seems significant because the waiter may have put the cyanide in the glass. But Christie goes to considerable lengths to establish that this cannot have been the case. The waiter's action, however, *is* the most significant point in the novel. We learn, at the big reveal, that he accidentally put the handbag at one place-setting removed from its original position. When the diners return to the table, they take their cue from the position of the handbag and sit one place removed from their original seat. This results in George Barton toasting Rosemary with the glass that had been intended for the person sitting next to him.

How can Christie help readers to see this crucial point in a way that is fair but not obvious? What she does is to craft a cunning clue by analogy. The three detectives in the novel – Anthony Browne, Chief Inspector Kemp and Colonel Race – are sitting at a small round marble-topped table drinking tea and coffee. At one point they all get up from the café table for a few minutes. When they return, Race takes a sip from his drink, but it is the wrong drink. Kemp takes a sip from his drink. Again it is not his drink. Anthony is amused. Suddenly his two companions understand what Anthony has done, and why. Christie is challenging the reader: can you see what Anthony's companions have suddenly realised?

Christie only occasionally makes use of analogy. Miss Marple, on the other hand, lives in a world of analogies. She appears to have a cast of mind that is quite different from Poirot's. Poirot, an immigrant with no clear sense of place or of belonging, thinks in an abstract and logical way. Marple, on the other hand, is firmly situated in St Mary Mead, with church and vicar, family doctor and manor. She has known most of her neighbours for many years. Unlike Poirot, Marple seldom needs to sit and think. She tends to see things almost immediately using her analogies in understanding human nature.

Are the plots, clues and misdirections influenced by the way each detective thinks? Do Marple's village life analogies help the reader solve the mysteries?

In *The Body in the Library* (1942) there are nine village life analogies. One enables Marple to identify which friend of the murdered girl guide has been lying. A further six tell us what we already know. Only two analogies give Miss Marple any insights relevant to the murder puzzle. The first occurs during a discussion of why the body of Ruby Keene was found in Colonel Bantry's library. The chief constable, Colonel Melchett, asks Miss Marple whether she has an explanation. Miss Marple's rather cryptic reply is to relate an anecdote about a frog that jumped out of a clock. This analogy helps Miss Marple but is of no help to the reader. The most significant of Marple's analogies is in chapter 1. After Marple has seen the body in the library, she tells her friend, Mrs Bantry, that she was reminded of a friend's daughter, Edie. The description of the dead woman does indeed provide both Miss Marple and the reader with significant clues, but the analogy with Edie plays no part.

No. The settings and *dramatis personae* are rather different in a Marple, compared with a Poirot, novel. The plots, clues and misdirections, however, are uninfluenced by the character of the detective. Miss Marple's analogies are an aspect of her character but are not relevant to the puzzle. Whether the detective is Poirot or Marple makes no difference to how the reader can solve the mystery.

CHAPTER SIXTEEN

Reflections and rotations

Using the mirror's gaze to reveal while concealing

Plot spoilers for: *After the Funeral*; *Dumb Witness*; *The Clocks*.

Agatha Christie was a lateral thinker years before Edward de Bono's book brought this idea to prominence. To solve a Christie puzzle the reader has to avoid the obvious route through her maze.

Christie enjoyed the ideas of mirrors and reflections to hint that things may be the opposite of what you assume. She finds ways to show how eyewitnesses can be mistaken in what they think they saw, just as Shakespeare fools characters in his comedies. Both authors make you doubt your eyes.

The importance of mirrors are reflected in Christie's titles: *The Mirror Crack'd from Side to Side* (1962), and *They Do It with Mirrors* (1952). *The Mirror Crack'd from Side to Side*, a quote from Tennyson, one of Christie's favourite poets, has masterful misdirections. In *They Do It with Mirrors* the entire plot is themed as a reflection of reality. Everything is the opposite of what it seems, distorted through a mirror, darkly. The clues, too, are the inverse, the reflection, of what they seem. In that novel, a philanthropist, Serracold, and his very rich wife have converted their country house into a boys' borstal. Serracold's passionate belief is that these criminal boys are not bad but mad. The idea behind the borstal is that if the boys are given psychological therapy they will be able to rehabilitate into society and lead good, useful lives. The Serracolds employ psychiatrists. A visitor is murdered and, of course, suspicion falls upon the criminal adolescents – but they are safely under lock and key at night. Or are they? The staff are sure they are all accounted for, but these boys will always find a way out. In this book it is the psychiatrists who are mad; the borstal boys are sane. The caring are callous, and a loving husband sends poisoned chocolates to his own wife with no intention of harming her. A canon's widow, a staunch Christian, is very critical and unforgiving of others' weaknesses. An outrageously flirty young woman is actually deeply in love with her husband. Serracold's secretary is feigning mental illness. As in Shakespeare's *Macbeth* 'Fair is foul and foul is fair' throughout the fabric of this tale.

The reader is given the different characters' reactions to the same occurrence, which contributes to the pervading feeling of unease and unpleasantness. When Serracold's secretary slams the door behind him, one person puts it down to bad manners, one to his being sensitive and a third to his being mad.

In *After the Funeral* (1953), Cora attends her brother's funeral. They had not been close, and the other family members and solicitor had not seen Cora for many years. It was her hairstyle and her behaviour that they found familiar: the way she peered through her fringe like a rather shy animal, her abrupt manner of talking and how she would bend her head to one side before saying something outrageous. Christie is telling us, but without drawing attention to the point, that what seemed recognisable about Cora were her mannerisms, that could be imitated, rather than her physical likeness. At the family gathering to discuss disposal of the deceased's belongings Cora puts her head to one side and suggests that her brother had been murdered. In true Christie fashion, Cora is the next to die. There was, however, something about Cora after the funeral which disturbed her sister-in-law. There is a discussion, apparently of no importance, about how we see ourselves in mirrors, always as a reversed image. This turns out to be an important clue with which to crack this Christie puzzle.

In *The Clocks* (1963) Christie uses a mirror metaphorically. One has to reflect in order to find the solution. Poirot works out what sort of man the dead person must have been, and who had murdered him, without ever knowing the corpse's identity. Poirot sits in his square armchair and puzzles the problem out, by reflection of thought. He exercises his little grey cells. The dashing young hero of the book, Colin Lamb, does all the groundwork. Poirot relies on Colin's meticulous verbatim interview reports to derive a solution. Poirot uses Lamb like he did Hastings, without sharing his suspicions with him. At the end of an interview with Poirot, Lamb asks about the strange business of the clocks. Poirot replies enigmatically by reciting a whole stanza from *The Walrus and the Carpenter*, which, crucially, is from *Alice Through the Looking Glass*, and simply asks Lamb to reflect upon it, without any other explanation! Poirot enjoyed hugging his clever thoughts to himself in a very maddening manner for Lamb and reader alike.

There is also a physical clue in *The Clocks* (1963), although it requires rotation rather than reflection. A British agent has died before the book begins, with a scrap of headed notepaper in his wallet, on which is written 61M together with a picture of a crescent. Lamb has been looking at all the pubs with moon or crescent in their name, and has now moved onto streets called Crescent, looking for a number 61, and for someone whose name begins with M. Eventually Lamb realises that the note was scribbled with the headed notepaper upside down. 61M becomes W19, and all the pieces fall into place.

In *Dumb Witness* (1937), there are two cousins, Theresa Arundell (TA) and Arabella Tanios (AT), who stand to inherit a vast fortune when their aged aunt dies. Both young women are in dire need of cash. Theresa adores well-cut, expensive clothes. We are told that Arabella copies Theresa's fashions. Their aunt is murdered. An eyewitness had previously seen a woman fixing a trip wire to the top of the stairs – the aunt does trip and fall but is not killed at that point. The witness saw, through her bedroom mirror, the woman kneeling on the staircase in her dark dressing gown. The gown was fastened with a silver brooch bearing the initials TA. This clue, like a mirror, deceives and reveals at the same time.

In *Third Girl* (1966) someone is murdered in a rather shoddily built modern block of flats. The person who is living in the flat below that of the victim comes to seek Poirot's help. The numbers of the flat doors keep falling off. The 76 of the victim's flat narrowly misses Poirot's patent-leather shoes. Mrs Oliver has to replace the 7 of 67 on their client's door. It looks as though Christie is going to use sleight of hand. One can see her playing with 67 and 76 – like AT and TA, and 61M and W19 in the examples above. But it turns out that she is playing with the reader who thinks he knows her.

In *Curtain* (1975) there is a physical rotational clue of another kind. Some guests are just about to have coffee after supper. The poured drinks are on a small coffee table that can be turned around, as it is also a mini library containing book shelving underneath. A murderer has poisoned one of the cups. The guests rush outside to see a shooting star before anyone has drunk the beverage. In this brief interlude, Hastings innocently rotates the coffee table, because he is looking for a copy of *Othello*. Hastings was absorbed finishing a crossword and uninterested in romantic shooting stars. The table looks exactly the same. Only Hastings knew he had rotated it by 180 degrees. All the guests troop back to sip their coffee. Someone dies...

Christie wrote many thrillers or adventure stories, as well as her better known whodunnits. In the adventure stories there is a more breathless narrative pace as the heroes are chased, or as they track down the villains. There is little time for thoughtful reflection. In *They Came to Baghdad* (1951) there is an exciting scene that could be straight out of a *James Bond*. It is a great thriller. A British secret agent is changing his clothes in a shop in Basrah. There is a big copper coffee pot, recently polished, on the shelf in front of him. The agent notices the gleam of a knife reflected in coffee pot. And so the agent narrowly escapes the assassin's blade, to fight another day.

CHAPTER SEVENTEEN

Spells and spellings

Words or grammar as hidden clues

Plot spoilers for: *A Murder Is Announced.*

Near the beginning of *The Man in the Brown Suit* (1924) there is a clue on a scrap of paper: a series of numbers (17.1 22) and the name Kilmorden Castle. In true thriller form this information is found near a corpse. It is dropped by a man, disguised in false beard and glasses, who searches the dead body before running off. Our heroine, Anne, sees the piece of paper drop from his hand. The clue highlights the ambiguities of a very simple message. Anne assumes it is a date – the 17th January 1922 – and a place to meet. Anne tries and fails to find out where Kilmorden Castle is located, and who lives there. By pure serendipity, Anne trudges by a shipping office and sees a model of a boat – the Kenilworth *Castle*. She realises that all the Castle Line ships have *Castle* in their name. She discovers that *Kilmorden Castle* is a passenger steamer, and that it is about to sail to Cape Town – on the 17th January.

With the panache of a dashing Christie adventuress Anne spends all her money on a first-class ticket. She is certain that she is now on the track of some mystery. Nothing happens on the 17th, except that Anne is dreadfully seasick, as Christie was herself when she sailed to South Africa in 1922. At Madeira Anne manages to change into cabin 17, still trying to puzzle out the ambiguity of the message, thinking perhaps that the 17 could be referring to the cabin number. Various people try to evict her from cabin 17. This re-enforces her belief that the 17 in the message must be about that cabin, rather than the date the ship sailed. Anne thinks hard and decides that the message means: cabin 17 at 1pm on the 22nd of the month. And the 22nd is, tomorrow!

And so the adventure continues. This is Christie at her feminist best, calmly showing that young women can think as rationally and logically as men. In the early 1920s when this book was written, unmarried women under thirty did not have the vote. It was not until 1928, that all women over the age of twenty-one in the United Kingdom gained equal voting rights with men. Women had to swallow a lot of verbal abuse in the course of a normal day. Christie captures perfectly the patronising sexism, that is still with us, in the character of the newspaper baron Lord Nasby. He tells Anne that he likes cheek from a pretty girl and that, for a woman, she is surprisingly accurate about time.

Christie was a social historian. She did not intend to be one, but she was a shrewd observer of everyday life and she set most of her novels at the time of writing. In reading her books in the order she wrote them we see how Britain changed from 1920 to 1970.

Born in 1890, Christie had a wealthy upper-class Victorian childhood in Torquay. She writes about butlers, cooks, parlour maids, house maids, chauffeurs and gardeners with fluency and often fondness: they were her childhood companions. Christie's older sister fulfilled her Victorian destiny by marrying a man with money and a title. Christie's father was swindled out of his money by his American trustees, and died when Miss Agatha Miller was only eleven years old. This left Miss Miller and her mother in much reduced circumstances. Quite often in the early Christie novels there is a feisty young girl and her mother who have come down in the world.

The 1920s books give up to date references to jazz, Diaghilev's Ballets Russes, and Einstein. The books of the 1930s have brave aviators circumnavigating the world, and the commercial airlines running from Paris to London. Writing in the 1940s Christie mentions the atomic bomb, fifth column spies, the Second World War and its terrible aftermath. In the 1950s she writes about council houses and the newly built holiday resorts that spoil the Devon coast. Char ladies replace the live-in domestic servants. In the swinging '60s there are trendy Kings Road coffee bars complete with sex, drugs and rock 'n' roll. Bets are taken on whether the Russians will be the first to put a man on the moon. Young women are increasingly independent, living in shared rented accommodation, and work for their living. There are mentions of gasworks, and garden gnomes. By the 1970s the inquisitive old ladies are now in old people's homes, rather than helpfully staring out of their own front windows all day long. By this stage in her writing Christie had travelled a very long road from her early novel with Clement Edward Alistair Brent, ninth Marquis of Caterham, and the owner of that magnificent Tudor ancestral country house: Chimneys.

A quarter of a century after *The Man in the Brown Suit* Christie wrote another of her adventure stories, *They Came to Baghdad* (1951). In that novel there is a misheard clue, given as a misspelling. The feisty young heroine, Victoria, hears the last words of a dying man who is clutching a red knitted scarf to his chest where he was stabbed. She thinks that he says someone's name, something French, possibly Lefarge. There is no character in the book with a name anything like *Lefarge*. In the previous chapter Christie described something Victoria says as a Micawber-like pronouncement. Christie does not patronise her readers; she does not tell us that Micawber is a character in *David Copperfield*. She expects her readers to share her knowledge of Shakespeare, Tennyson and, in this instance, Dickens. There is a second, and much later, reference to Dickens. Victoria is hiding out at an archaeological dig in the desert with very little light fiction to amuse her. But *A Tale of Two Cities* is on the bookshelf. She did not know the book. She starts to read and suddenly realises that the dying words must have been *Defarge*. Victoria puts the two halves of the misspelt clue together and realises why that man was stabbed in the heart, and where the secret code is hidden. These clues are not really meant to be solved by the reader. As in a Sherlock Holmes story, they are fun for the reader and they show the intelligence of the characters.

They Came to Baghdad is one of the very few Christie novels that has not yet been adapted for the screen. It deserves to be filmed. Although not a whodunnit it is a good story and a great read: its brilliance seems not to be fully appreciated. It is also vivid and funny. Christie enjoyed herself describing various archaeologists and their absent-mindedness about practical aspects of daily living because they are obsessed with the far past. Christie often stayed with her second husband, Max Mallowan, when he was working on the digs in Mesopotamia.

Brief cryptic messages and misspellings were, of course, part and parcel of adventure stories long before Christie started writing. What Christie did, in her whodunnit novels, was to turn them into genuine clues that a reader could use to help solve the puzzle.

Christie borrows, probably from Conan Doyle, the idea that a word can change its meaning if part is missing. The most simple transformation is the word *she* to *he*, which Christie uses to good effect in *Lord Edgware Dies* (1933).

In *Sad Cypress* (1940) the transformation is rather more esoteric. One of the district nurses in that novel reports that a tube of morphine has been stolen. The printed label is reproduced in the novel as a facsimile with the torn paper edges visible. The inference is that this label was from the stolen tube of morphine. The subtle point which we missed, even though we have seen morphine ampoules for over forty years in our work as doctors, is that on a bottle of morphine, the word 'Morphine' was, and still is, printed with a capital M. The clue is that on the torn label it is clear that if the torn word is morphine then the initial 'm' is lower case and not upper case. For Christie, with her proof-reader's eye and her training as an apothecary's assistant during the First World War, this is a fair clue. For most of the rest of us the clue depends on rather too much knowledge. Especially as we need to deduce what the drug in the tube really was, *and* what it is used for.

It is not until *A Murder Is Announced* (1950) that Christie has fully developed her *spells and spellings*. This novel is a tale of two sisters. Miss Letitia Blacklock, Letty, had been a successful secretary. Her sister, Miss Charlotte Blacklock, Lotty, has sadly died of natural causes before the story begins. Only one vowel stands to differentiate the two sisters when people talk about them. Dora Bunner, who was a friend of both sisters, is a wittering elderly lady, rather like Miss Marple but without that steely core. Bunner is being ruthlessly pumped by Marple for information. In the course of the conversation, or interrogation, Bunner refers to Lotty when she should have said Letty. Readers are unlikely to notice that Dora used the wrong name, and perhaps it is simply a mistake. Or perhaps not.

There is another spelling clue later in the novel. Inspector Craddock shows Miss Marple a letter from Letitia Blacklock to her sister, in which Letty wrote the word *enquiring*. In a more recent note from Letitia Blacklock, written after the death of her sister, she wrote the word *inquiries*.

There are further plays on words which Christie uses both as clue and misdirection. Pip and Emma are twins who might inherit a fortune. They have not been heard of since they were children and must now be adult. Inspector Craddock assumes that Pip is a boy, like Pip in Dickens' *Great Expectations*. Shortly after we have heard about Pip and Emma we are introduced to Mrs Phillipa Haymes.

In *The Clocks* (1963) Christie uses grammar to set a somewhat mediocre clue. A year earlier, however, in *The Mirror Crack'd from Side to Side* (1962), Christie was far more sophisticated. Miss Marple talks, apparently inconsequentially, about a parlourmaid whose grammar was bad and who would use pronouns in most confusing ways. As so often with Christie, what seems inconsequential hides a valuable clue. The clue here is that there is someone else in the novel whose grammar was bad. The grammar in that case misleads the detectives and probably most readers, but the reader who realises that the grammar was bad will understand a vital clue. The clue makes use of the ways in which we can misuse grammar in ordinary conversation. It could also be seen as an example of a clue by analogy since Miss Marple's parlourmaid speaks in a way that is analogous to someone else. It is also a clue that has been sawn into two halves.

CHAPTER EIGHTEEN

Sawing the clue in half

Placing the two halves of a single clue in different parts
of the book

Plot spoilers for: *After the Funeral*; *The Clocks*.

When we were children magicians who appeared on
television fascinated us. There was glamour, sparkle
and excitement. We could never work out how magicians
sawed their lovely assistants in half, or why they went to
all that bother, when the assistant was clearly whole again
by the end of the trick. It worried us that the magician
had a huge fixed fake smile whilst sawing away, as did his
assistant despite the atrocity enacted upon her. It seemed
wrong on so many levels.

Agatha Christie is the opposite of these commercial
stage magicians. One of her best tricks is to saw her clues
in half, stealthily burying the pieces in her text, sometimes
over a hundred pages apart. No razzmatazz, just pure
skill. As a reader you will come across odd nuggets of
information in her books that you have to hoard and
remember, like a squirrel collecting nuts in autumn.

At the end of every chapter you can reflect on what you have gleaned. Some of it will become useful; most will be irrelevant to the kernel of the plot. Quite suddenly, like Victoria in *They Came to Baghdad* (1951) (chapter 17), you get that truly magical flash of lightning when two halves of a clue stick together in your head, and the bones of the plot are revealed.

There is a good example of a clue sawn, not into half but into thirds, in *After the Funeral* (1953). The family members gather, like vultures, at Enderby Hall for the reading of Richard Abernethie's will. One of them, we are told on page 14 of the Fontana edition, is looking at some wax flowers that are displayed on a malachite table. On page 153, Helen lifts the protective glass shade from the wax flowers. At that moment she is startled by a question from Poirot and drops and breaks the glass shade. Helen decides to put the undamaged wax flowers in a cupboard to protect them until she can order a replacement glass dome. By page 192 the family members are fighting over who takes this malachite table home. One of those present, Miss Gilchrist, who is not one of the family, says that the wax flowers looked perfect on the malachite table. The question is, how did Miss Gilchrist know the flowers looked so right on the table when she had never set foot in Enderby Hall before?

In *The Clocks* an unknown body of a man is found in a blind woman's home. The police go from house to house questioning all the neighbours for information. Early in the novel we learn that after her great-uncle died Mrs Bland is the only one of her family left. Fifty-six pages later, Mrs Bland says that her sister lives near her. The reader needs to be alert and have a good memory to spot the inconsistencies that can reveal the secret of the plot. We completely missed this nugget of information.

The difficulty for the reader when a clue is 'sawn in half' is to notice and remember the first piece of information so that it can be combined with the subsequent piece of information. If the two (or more) parts of the clue are remembered then the clue is generally obvious.

Another of Christie's methods is to plant clues that even if remembered do not give any insights unless they are combined with one or more further clues. In other words, Christie creates *clue clusters*. This requires the reader to put the shards of clues together and then assemble them into a logical pattern. As Dr Leidner says in *Murder in Mesopotamia* (1936), Poirot is so good at doing this that he could have been an archaeologist.

CHAPTER NINETEEN

Clue clusters

Several clues fall into place with a leap of insight

Plot spoilers for: *After the Funeral.*

Christie's brilliance in clueing lies not only in her use of a wide variety of types but also in the way that her clues relate to each other. In most of her novels she creates *clue clusters*: a number of clues, each one of which is insufficient to solve the puzzle, but taken together, and with an act of insight, they fall into place.

These clue clusters require us to think in a quite different way from, for example, deductive clues (chapter 14). With deductive clues we have to carefully consider the implications of a single clue: what it tells us about the solution. The movement is from clue to solution. With clue clusters our thinking goes in the opposite direction: from solution to clues. Sometimes we suddenly see the solution through an act of inspiration and see that it accounts for the clues. Sometimes we will go carefully through various possible solutions and see which best fits the clue clusters.

To give an example. A key element in the plot of *After the Funeral* (1953) is that, after the death of Cora, Miss Gilchrist inherits a painting that appears to be worthless but is in fact valuable (chapter 3). Christie provides us with a cluster of *eight* clues:

1. Cora buys paintings cheaply at local sales in the hope of picking up a bargain.
2. One of Cora's hobbies is to paint pictures of seaside resorts. These paintings are not very good and look rather like picture postcards. Miss Gilchrist insists, however, that Cora never copied postcards and always painted from life.
3. On one occasion Cora believes that she may have bought a Rembrandt at a local sale. The art critic, Mr Guthrie, is asked to give an opinion. The painting is nothing like a Rembrandt and is essentially worthless. As an aside Mr Guthrie says that a Cuyp had recently been bought cheaply at a farmhouse sale.
4. Miss Gilchrist's eyes rest with particular fondness on a painting by Cora of Polflexan Harbour.
5. We learn, however, that the painting of Polflexan Harbour must have been painted from a postcard because it shows a pier that was destroyed before the picture was painted.
6. When, just after the murder, the family solicitor, Mr Entwhistle, visits the cottage where Miss Gilchrist lived with Cora there is a strong smell of oil paint.
7. As an aside we are told that Miss Gilchrist's father was a painter and Miss Gilchrist herself can paint.

8. After Cora's death Miss Gilchrist successfully pleads with the family solicitor that she can have Cora's painting of Polflexan Harbour as a souvenir.

None of these clues is substantial in itself. A reader, however, who hits on the idea that Cora did indeed buy a genuinely valuable painting at a local sale, and that Miss Gilchrist painted a picture, taken from a postcard, of Polflexan Harbour over it, will realise that this is correct. This key element of the plot passes what might be called the *cryptic crossword test*: the puzzle is not easy to work out but the clues ensure that those who hit on the right solution can be pretty certain that they have done so.

Clue clusters are challenging because they require an act of insight. One of the difficulties for the reader is that it is not obvious that any of the eight clues above *is* a clue. It is only when they are considered together that they can be seen for what they are. Christie compounds the problem by sometimes planting *false* clues. False clues are neither clues to the main plot nor to any of the red-herring plots. They sound, however, as though they should be clues and so readers will try to fit them into the puzzle. For example, in *A Murder Is Announced* (1950) after Murgatroyd and Hinchcliffe have been interviewed by the police, following the first murder, Murgatroyd asks Hinchcliffe whether she was very awful. Hinchcliffe replies that she did very well. This is enigmatic and suspicious but in fact is innocent. It turns out that Hinchcliffe is simply reassuring her friend.

The kind of thinking that clue clusters require is

similar to that often needed in medical diagnosis, and indeed in science more generally. A patient, for example, has a number of signs and symptoms suggestive of disease. Rather like a jigsaw puzzle these signs and symptoms have to be put together to form a coherent picture – the diagnosis. The problem can be made more difficult by the fact that some of the signs and symptoms may be irrelevant to the main diagnosis – false clues. It is as though some of the pieces are from a different jigsaw. Once an initial diagnosis is made it is easy to stop thinking. Any new signs and symptoms are fitted into that diagnosis. A good doctor needs to keep flexible, with an open mind, and to continue reviewing all the evidence. The same is true when we read an Agatha Christie whodunnit. It is all too easy to alight on a solution early and then squeeze new information into that solution. Christie makes use of this tendency by encouraging us to decide on the solution before we have been given all the clues.

The analogy of the jigsaw puzzle is from Poirot. Mrs Gardener, in *Evil Under the Sun* (1941), is one of Christie's rather silly women who contributes to the comedy rather than to the plot. At one point she is trying to solve a jigsaw puzzle. She has a piece that is white and thinks that it must be part of a rug. But Poirot tells her that it is part of the cat. Mrs Gardener contradicts him saying that the cat is black. Poirot agrees but realises that the black cat has a white tip to its tail. A while later when Poirot is trying to solve the murder mystery he thinks to himself how difficult it is to know which pieces belong to the fur rug and which to the cat's tail.

In *Evil Under the Sun* we see a Poirot rather more interested in sex than in any other novel. In the TV episode of *The Chocolate Box* starring David Suchet (1993), based on the 1923 short story of the same name, there is a suggestion that Poirot is enamoured of Virginie Mesnard (played by Anna Chancellor). Suchet's Poirot throughout the series wears the buttonhole ornament she gave him. This, though, is an invention of the TV scriptwriters and is not evident in Christie's story. We do sense that Poirot is mildly attracted to Katherine Grey in *The Mystery of the Blue Train* (1928). There is the Countess Vera Rossakoff whom we first meet in *The Big Four* (1927). Poirot mentions her admiringly in *One, Two, Buckle My Shoe* (1940) rather as Holmes talks of Irene Adler. It is only the effect of Lady Edgware's sexual charms (in *Lord Edgware Dies*, 1933) that can account for Poirot taking on the role of divorce broker at her request. In *Evil Under the Sun*, however, Poirot's attraction to women is more blatant. Perhaps it is the sun, the sand and the scantily clad young women that put Poirot in the mood.

Early in the novel Poirot, uncharacteristically, engages in a conversation about women with the crude, almost lewd, Major Barry. Poirot says that in his youth it was rare for a woman to show more than the ankle. He then says how alluring might be the glimpse of a petticoat, the contour of the calf, a knee, a garter... Fortunately Poirot proceeds no further on this anatomical journey.

When Arlena Marshall arrives Hercule Poirot's moustache quivers appreciatively. He is sufficiently taken with her to immerse his white suede shoes in the sea to help her to sail off to what is her fateful rendezvous. It is not the rather stupid Arlena, however, who takes his main fancy. It is Rosamund Darnley. Indeed he admits that he admired Rosamund Darnley as much as any woman he had ever met. He likes her figure, the way she holds herself, her hair, her smile. On passing her room he stops to imbibe the sense of her personality.

Rosamund Darnley has created a successful dressmaking business in London. She suggests to Poirot that, like all men, he believes that women can only be content if they are married and are mothers. Poirot, however, replies saying that only one woman in a thousand can achieve what she has done: to make a name and a position for herself. One feels Poirot's admiration and respect for a woman who, like Christie, of course, can make a successful career for herself. The novel's ending, therefore, is tinged with sadness. As with so many of Christie's novels, after the denouement there is a final tying up of a romance that had been brewing through the book. This time it is the romance between Rosamund and the victim's husband Kenneth Marshall. If Poirot had ever entertained a hope of a romantic relationship with Rosamund these hopes are now dashed.

For the modern reader Rosamund's final words are rather shocking. In what is effectively his proposal of marriage, Kenneth Marshall tells Rosamund to give up her business and live with him in the country. She at first replies with proper feistiness telling him that he has a nerve to tell her to give up all that she has achieved. But he forces her to choose between him and her business. Sadly she chooses him. Perhaps she would have had a more fulfilled life as the wife of Hercule Poirot.

CHAPTER TWENTY

Dr Jekyll and Mr Hyde

The narrator as character lies; the narrator as narrator
tells the truth

Plot spoilers for: *The Murder of Roger Ackroyd*.

In Stevenson's story, Dr Jekyll and Mr Hyde are two
manifestations of the same person: Dr Jekyll apparently
good, a kindly hard-working physician; Mr Hyde evil. Dr
Jekyll, however, transforms himself into Mr Hyde in order
to carry out evil acts, murder included, without the risk
of sullying his reputation as Dr Jekyll. In Christie's novel,
The Murder of Roger Ackroyd (1926), Dr Sheppard, the
kindly hard-working family doctor, is a blackmailer and a
murderer. But Dr Sheppard is also the narrator of the story.
As narrator he seeks to conceal his evil nature from us.

After the publication of *The Murder of Roger Ackroyd*
many readers thought that Christie had cheated. To cheat
there must be rules. The 'rule' that Christie had broken was
that in a whodunnit the narrator cannot be the murderer.

In these more knowing times authors play games with
the relationships between reader, writer and narrator.

Pierre Bayard, French psychoanalyst and professor of literature, is best known for *How to Talk About Books You Haven't Read*. His earlier book, *Who Killed Roger Ackroyd?*, was published in 2000. Although we haven't read it, we believe that Bayard argues that Christie was deceived by Dr Sheppard, her own narrator. According to Bayard Dr Sheppard was not in fact the murderer. Sheppard deceives Christie and the reader in order to protect his beloved sister, Caroline. If Christie can be deceived in this way, however, there is a more worrying possibility. Both Poirot's and Miss Marple's presence at the scenes of so many murders cannot be coincidence. If we are to re-read Christie in the footsteps of Bayard we must look beyond the individual novel and examine the broader patterns. We may find that both detectives have outsmarted readers and author alike.

The Murder of Roger Ackroyd invites these post-modern musings because it plays with the reader's assumptions about the narrator. It was Christie's brother-in-law, James Watts, and Lord Mountbatten, the last Viceroy of India, who independently suggested to Christie the central idea for the plot. Christie had, in fact, already used the idea in a small way. A part of her 1924 novel *The Man in the Brown Suit* is written by the perpetrator. That novel, however, is more adventure story than whodunnit, and we are not dependent on the perpetrator's narrative for the clues. *The Murder of Roger Ackroyd*, in contrast, is a whodunnit in which the whole narrative is written by the murderer.

Solving a whodunnit depends on our being given the correct facts. The narrator must be reliable. So how can it be fair to the reader for the narrator to be the murderer? Christie solves the problem through a brilliant central idea: the narrator as narrator tells the truth; the narrator as a character sometimes lies. There remains a problem. How can the narrator conceal the murder without lying? The answer is that he is sometimes economical with the truth. He does not tell us, for example, that he kills Roger Ackroyd. Neither is he entirely open about what he is thinking. All narrators select what they do and don't tell the reader. Omission of information is not a problem as long as the solution is fairly clued.

Ackroyd is very well clued, and there are two quite different types of clue. There is the type shared with most whodunnits – clues available both to the reader and the detective within the novel. There are also clues almost unique to this novel – what might be called 'narrative clues'. In a brilliant move Christie turned the narrator's economy with the truth into clues for the reader. These are generally rather enigmatic statements: statements that a story-teller like Hastings or Watson would never make. It is easy to overlook these clues, to consider that they are slightly odd phrases. This trail of narrative clues, however, has that hallmark of the mature Christie: none of the strange phrasings by itself can lead directly to the solution, but if the correct solution is seriously considered they fall into place.

On the night of the murder Dr Sheppard has dinner at Ackroyd's house. After dinner the two men go to Ackroyd's study. Parker, Ackroyd's butler, brings in a letter that has just been delivered – the letter that could expose Sheppard as a blackmailer. Sheppard asks Ackroyd to read the letter – presumably to see whether he is exposed. Ackroyd says that he will read the letter later. Christie then takes us right to the moment of the murder. In a brilliant paragraph Sheppard describes the moment, just after committing the murder, as he leaves Ackroyd's study and looks round the room to check that he has done what he had planned.

The murder has taken place between the lines of that paragraph. Our narrator withholds information, but although he conceals, he also reveals. At the start of the novel Dr Sheppard is called to a patient, Mrs Ferrars. She is dead – an overdose of tranquillisers, probably suicide. We soon learn that Mrs Ferrars had murdered her husband a year earlier and that she was being blackmailed by an unknown person. Sheppard tells us that when he had last seen Mrs Ferrars her manner had been normal enough, considering the circumstances, but he does not enlarge, as most narrators would have done, on what exact circumstances he has in mind.

A paragraph later when Sheppard is remembering having seen Ralph Paton (Ackroyd's nephew) and Mrs Ferrars talking very earnestly together he tells us that this is when he first felt a foreboding of the future. The reader could understand him to mean a foreboding that Ackroyd would be murdered, but the phrasing does not quite fit that interpretation.

Two chapters later Roger Ackroyd says to Dr Sheppard that Mrs Ferrars is being blackmailed. Sheppard is again enigmatic. He tells us that he suddenly sees, in his mind's eye, Ralph Paton and Mrs Ferrars talking earnestly together and that he gets a pang of anxiety. He starts to tell us why he feels anxious but stops in mid-sentence and is then reassured by remembering that Ralph Paton seemed open and friendly towards him later that day. The reason for Sheppard's anxiety is that he wonders whether Mrs Ferrars had told Ralph Paton that Sheppard was blackmailing her.

Just after he has murdered Ackroyd, Sheppard returns to his own house, which he shares with his sister Caroline. Caroline wonders why Sheppard has come back home so early. Sheppard tells us that in trying to satisfy Caroline's curiosity he had to somewhat distort the truth. And when Sheppard goes back to Ackroyd's house later that evening he enters Ackroyd's study, sends Ackroyd's butler, Parker, to call the police and is left alone in the room with Ackroyd's dead body. He tells us that he did what he had to do. An astute reader might wonder what he means – why did he have to do anything?

Two thirds of the way through the book Poirot describes to Sheppard and his sister, Caroline, how a decent man might become a blackmailer and then a murderer. It is an accurate account of how Sheppard followed exactly this path, although Christie misdirects the reader into thinking that Poirot is referring to Ralph Paton. After Poirot's speech Sheppard writes that Poirot's analysis struck fear into both himself and his sister. The fear for Sheppard is that Poirot knows he is the murderer. For the loyal Caroline this is probably the moment when she first, however fleetingly, has an inkling of what her brother has done.

In order to make sure that she is being fair to the reader Christie gives two clues that Sheppard the narrator omits relevant information. Sheppard visits the Three Boars on the way to Ackroyd's house and before he has committed the murder. He meets with Ralph Paton. As narrator he is quite open about this. Later Poirot asks Sheppard why he went to the Three Boars on his way home, at night. Sheppard has to think carefully before replying and then says that he wanted to inform Ralph Paton about his uncle's death. This visit to the Three Boars cannot, however, have been the one that the narrator told us about because that visit was, crucially, before Ackroyd had been murdered. Christie has given us the information needed to realise that Sheppard has not been open about all that he did on that fateful night.

The second clue is near the end of the book after Poirot has read Sheppard's account of the case (i.e. most of the book that we are reading). Poirot ironically compliments Sheppard on his modesty – on how he has been so reticent in detailing his own role in the events that he has related.

In these ways Christie turns the issue of the narrator being also the murderer from a problem into an opportunity. She creates a new class of clue, a class that she will hardly ever need again.

The Murder of Roger Ackroyd was Christie's third Poirot novel. It posed, as we have seen, considerable narrative problems because of its solution. In solving these problems Christie wove together plot, clues and misdirections. She had found both her voice and her metier.

CHAPTER TWENTY-ONE

The wood, not the trees

Using the whole theme or structure of the novel as an
overarching clue

Plot spoilers for: *Three Act Tragedy*; *Death Comes as the End*.

Christie sometimes uses the theme of the entire novel
as a clue, like a cloth shot through with glittering gold.
The warp and the weft of the plot are tightly woven into
the clue structure. This makes for a satisfying read. Few
whodunnit writers manage such seamless integration of
clues with the overarching theme.

One example is *They Do It with Mirrors* (1952). The
idea of reflections runs through this novel (chapter 16).
Almost everything is the opposite of what it seems. By
understanding this the murders can be solved in one
intuitive leap.

Another example is *Three Act Tragedy* (1934), the
most theatrical of Christie's novels. The book is divided
into three acts and the theme of drama runs throughout.
Two of the characters are actors and one is a playwright.
The first death happens as though on stage, the main

characters gathered together in one room. This theatrical structure of the novel is neither arbitrary nor whimsical. The structure of the novel and the solution to the mystery form a unity. The novel is theatrical because the murders have been devised and carried out by a charismatic actor. We are told that Sir Charles Cartwright is always acting: he never simply leaves a room; he makes an exit.

It is possible to solve *Three Act Tragedy* simply by being sensitive to Christie's artistry. Structure and plot go hand in hand. Sir Charles is in the tradition of the great actor-managers: he is the central character and the director of the novel, the star part.

Christie was herself a highly successful playwright. *The Mousetrap*, its title taken from *Hamlet*, has had the longest continuous run of any play. It was vanquished, but only for a time, by the Covid-19 pandemic in 2020 just as Shakespeare's Globe Theatre was closed in 1608 by the bubonic plague.

Christie's novels and plays are full of Shakespeare quotes, or allusions to characters, most often to Lady Macbeth, Ophelia and Iago. But the influence of Shakespeare goes deeper. Christie often employs stratagems for misdirection similar to those used in Shakespeare's comedies. In Shakespeare it is the characters on stage who are deceived when the audience is in the know, as in a gulling scene. The audience laugh at the ignorant characters being made to look ridiculous. Christie uses gulling scenes created from false letters, or mistaken identities, to hoodwink the reader. Christie and her detectives have the last laugh.

In a few novels Christie uses a title taken from Shakespeare to give an arch and overarching clue to a novel's plot. For example, *Taken at the Flood* (1948), is a line in *Julius Caesar*. Christie's novel is about reckless audacity, like Brutus and Cassius' ill-fated Roman coup after murdering Caesar. *Sad Cypress* is about a jilted woman so miserable she willingly prepares to be hanged despite being innocent. The song in *Twelfth Night* from which the title is taken is about unrequited love leading through hopeless grief to death. These titles can act as theme clues, or at least hints: the wood rather than an individual tree. In another novel, *Sleeping Murder* (1976), it is *The Duchess of Malfi* – a play by Shakespeare's near contemporary, John Webster – that provides both a dramatic scene near the beginning of the novel and a pointer to the murderer for those who know the play.

Christie's debt to Shakespeare is greatest, however, in *Curtain: Poirot's Last Case* (1975) and in *Death Comes as the End* (1944). The central plot in each of these novels is taken directly from a Shakespeare tragedy. In the case of *Death Comes as the End* from *Macbeth*.

Death Comes as the End is Christie's most unusual book, set in Ancient Thebes rather than Ancient Scotland. In writing this Christie was something of a pioneer. A year earlier, in 1943, the American writer, Lillian de la Torre, published the first volume of her engaging short stories in which she imagines Samuel Johnson as an eighteenth-century Sherlock Holmes with James Boswell his Dr Watson. In 1949, the Dutch diplomat, scholar and writer, Robert van Gulik, brought the Chinese crime stories written in the eighteenth century, but set in the seventh century, to the attention of Western audiences. From 1951 van Gulik published his own charming detective novels, starring Judge Dee, which he also set in seventh-century China. It was not until the 1970s that the historical crime novel took off, particularly with the popular *Cadfael Chronicles* by Ellis Peters. Christie had been there thirty years earlier: *Death Comes as the End* may be the first historical whodunnit novel.

In Shakespeare's play it is Lady Macbeth who first suggests killing the King. When her husband refuses she upbraids him. In *Death Comes as the End*, Satipy encourages her husband, Yahmose, and his brother Sobek, to kill Nofret. When they hesitate Satipy's speech accusing them of having milk in their veins echoes Lady Macbeth.

Yahmose, like Macbeth, at first refuses to carry out the murder, but eventually caves in to the bullying. In *Macbeth*, Lady Macbeth is driven mad with guilt at what they have done. She sleepwalks. Her doctor says:

Infected minds
To their deaf pillows will discharge their secrets.

In *Death Comes as the End*, after Nofret's murder, the strident Satipy, just like Lady Macbeth, slowly goes to pieces. Satipy also talks in her sleep. Yahmose becomes worried that Satipy will confess. We never know how Lady Macbeth dies. We do, however, learn that Satipy plunges to her death off a cliff path.

Perhaps Christie was so busy meticulously researching the details and customs of Thebes in 2000 BC that she turned to Shakespeare for an off-the-peg plot. But then Shakespeare got much of his plot from Holinshed's *Chronicles of Scotland*.

James Thurber's humorous short story *The Macbeth Murder Mystery* appeared in the *New Yorker* magazine in October 1937. In a rather brilliant twist one of the characters who is a devotee of detective fiction buys *The Tragedy of Macbeth* not realising that it is a Shakespeare play. She reads it, hoping that it is like an Agatha Christie whodunnit. She puts forward her own solution to the murder of Duncan. It cannot have been Macbeth – that solution is too obvious!

Macbeth inspired some of the characters, but not the plot, in one of Christie's later novels, *The Pale Horse* (1961). The story begins after the hero has seen *Macbeth* at the Old Vic in London. He discusses with his friends over a post-theatre supper how they would produce the play. They agree that the three witches are overdone almost to the point of comic pantomime. They would be much more scary if they were just ordinary old women living in a country village. The novel then moves to a quiet, ordinary country village, Much Deeping, with three sly old women living in a former pub – The Pale Horse. The idea that evil can lurk in a seemingly idyllic English village is one of the overarching themes of the various Miss Marple novels.

Neither Miss Marple nor Hercule Poirot appear in *The Pale Horse*. It is, however, the one novel that connects their two worlds. Ariadne Oliver, who accompanies Poirot on several of his adventures, is a character in this novel. The vicar of Much Deeping, the Reverend Caleb Dane Calthrop and his wife Maude, are also in the story. They have appeared much earlier as friends of Miss Jane Marple in *The Moving Finger* (1942). *The Pale Horse* proves that Jane Marple and Hercule Poirot inhabit the same fictional space.

CHAPTER TWENTY-TWO

Criminal psychological profiling

Fitting the nature of the crime to the psychology of the
killer

Plot spoilers for: *Crooked House.*

In Christie's first published novel, *The Mysterious Affair
at Styles* (1920), Poirot mentions psychology only
once. His focus is on physical clues. In the second Poirot
novel, *The Murder on the Links* (1923), he uses the word
psychology, or its derivatives, seven times. In that novel
Poirot distinguishes between the type of detective who is
a trained observer of physical clues, and himself who is
most interested in the psychology of the case.

Poirot does not elaborate on what he means by
psychology. At this point in his development it seems to
refer to a person's behaviour. Poirot does hint, however, at
a more profound sense of the importance of psychology in
solving a crime – the possibility of understanding the brain,
or the mind, of the criminal from a study of the crimes.

That hint – knowing the mind of man – remains
dormant. In the ten years from 1926 to 1936 Christie

wrote several of her greatest whodunnits, developing her particularly sophisticated approach to plots and clues. Many of those clues involve how people behave or what they say. They are clues because, for example, someone reveals that they know something that they shouldn't know, or they behave in a way that doesn't make sense... unless... But they are not psychological in that more profound sense of revealing the mind of the murderer.

And then in 1936 Christie published *Cards on the Table*, the first novel in which we meet one of Christie's best characters, the fictional crime writer Mrs Ariadne Oliver. *Cards on the Table* was a bold experiment that didn't quite come off. Christie was attempting a new approach to clueing – a new kind of whodunnit. Her experiment is so interesting, the set-up so good and the character of Mrs Ariadne Oliver such fun, that we like this novel better than many that have a more satisfying solution.

Christie in a most unusual piece of writing outlines the entire plot for *Cards on the Table* in *The A.B.C. Murders* (1936), published earlier the same year. She had already placed her cards on the table before the book was published. Christie knew that she was trying something original and was worried that readers would not appreciate it. She took the unusual step of providing a foreword for *Cards on the Table*. In that foreword she tells us that we must solve the puzzle using psychology because what is of most interest is the mind of the murderer. She seems a little unsure whether this psychological approach works because she tells us that it was one of Poirot's favourite cases, although Hastings found it dull.

At the centre of the novel is the aesthete Mr Shaitana. He is a collector of fine things: Chinese furniture, Persian rugs, Japanese prints and murderers. He believes that a murderer who is supremely good at murder can be an artist. But a murderer who is caught is a failure. He invites to dinner, and a game of bridge, four people whom he thinks have got away with murder – they are part of his collection of fine things.

What Christie was attempting was to set the reader the task of identifying the murderer by matching the nature of the murder to the mind of one, and only one, of the suspects. Hence Christie's decision to make it crystal-clear who the suspects are and limiting their number to four.

Christie provides three sources of information to help the reader build up the psychological profiles of the four suspects. First, how they play bridge. Second, their past, and in particular the details around the deaths which may in each case have been murder. Third, the answers they give Poirot when he asks them to describe the contents of the room in which they played bridge.

Christie was in effect writing a novel about criminal psychological profiling over fifty years before it became popular in fiction in books, films and TV dramas (such as *The Silence of the Lambs* and *Criminal Minds*), and over thirty years before the first unit devoted to such an approach was set up in the FBI in 1972. Perhaps Christie knew about the attempt to use such an approach in the Jack the Ripper case in London in the 1880s. Perhaps it was simply the outcome of her developing the idea of psychological clues in a whodunnit.

This experiment in psychological profiling failed as a whodunnit. No reader can be confident in identifying the murderer on the basis of matching the suspects' psychologies to the nature of the murder. More definitive clues are needed. But Christie did not give up on exploring the nature and possibilities of psychological clues. Her creative mind kept thinking about the possibilities.

In *Appointment with Death* (1938) Christie explored the idea that the crime can be solved through an understanding of the psychology of the *victim*, rather than that of the murderer. At the beginning of the denouement, which stretches to almost 20% of the novel, Poirot promises that his reasoning will be mainly psychological. Carbury, the no-nonsense military Englishman, responds with a sigh – psychology is definitely not his thing. Despite Poirot's rhetoric, however, it is the factual clues that are the key to the solution. Psychological profiling once again failed to provide the basis for a convincing whodunnit. Christie gave up on the idea. Then in 1949 she published *Crooked House*. This is a highly original whodunnit wrapped inside a romantic cover. The nature of the solution posed narrative problems. As a by-product of solving these narrative problems, Christie wrote her most successful novel that involves the reader in criminal psychological profiling.

She again wrote a foreword. She wrote that she had saved this book up for years. What Christie had been thinking about was, presumably, how to write a *whodunnit* in which the murderer is a child as young as eleven or twelve years. She well knew that unless she was careful readers would say that the solution was unfair. It would be insufficient justification to respond that some children aged eleven years have, in fact, committed murder. Christie knew that she would have to make it psychologically plausible that the specific child, Josephine, would commit the murders. In making it plausible that Josephine *could* be the murderer she provides most of the evidence that Josephine *is* the murderer. There are a few conventional clues but they are insufficient to identify Josephine as the murderer with any degree of certainty. A reader, however, who notices the ways in which Christie suggests a child is capable of murder will realise that Josephine is the killer.

In the key scene the narrator, Charles Hayward, a man in his thirties, is talking to his father, who is Assistant Commissioner of Scotland Yard. He asks his father what murderers are like. In the course of his long and thoughtful answer, Charles' father provides grounds for believing that a child might commit murder. He says that the brake that operates with most of us to prevent us from killing doesn't operate with murderers. He goes on to adumbrate his views on the development of moral sensitivity: first children learn that things are wrong in the sense that they will be punished if they do them. Later they develop a true moral sense and feel that certain things are wrong. In this scene Christie does most of the groundwork of preparing the reader for a child murderer. But not all. Towards the end of the book Josephine's brother, Eustace, who is fifteen years old, is seriously considered as the possible murderer. It is not that large a step to then wonder about his younger sister.

In addition to the general clues that a child might be the murderer Christie sketches Josephine's character. We see her as precocious, arrogant and egotistical, and as treating the murders of her grandfather and nannie as rather fun – as excuses for an enjoyable game of sleuthing.

So has Christie made the solution too obvious? At each point where she provides the reader with grounds for considering Josephine the murderer she distracts the reader's attention. Charles' father uses the discussion of the moral development of children not to make the point that children can murder but that adult murderers are morally immature. Our attention is focussed on thinking which adults in the story might fit that description. At the end of the conversation Charles' father puts us off the scent and tells his son to make sure that the murderer does not kill Josephine.

Christie can get away with what might otherwise be clues that are too obvious because of her extraordinary skills at misdirection.

MISDIRECTIONS

CHAPTER TWENTY-THREE

Buried in froth

Clues hidden in padding

Plot spoilers for: *The Clocks*.

Two elderly ladies – Miss Marple and Dora Bunner – gossip amongst the yellow cakes and pink aprons of The Bluebird Tearooms. They witter on about their rheumatism and sciatica and other such trivia – on and on for over eighteen pages. Efficient readers will skim to the next chapter. There is, however, no part of *A Murder Is Announced* (1950) that rewards close reading more than this cosy scene. On five occasions Dora Bunner gives away significant clues but, so buried in the froth of her wittering, that they are almost invisible.

Christie never allowed success to lead to that inflation in word count that many popular writers find irresistible. Almost all her novels are between 55,000 and 75,000 words. The chapters are short, the pace fast, and she knows all the tricks to keep the pages turning. Every chapter in a Christie novel has purpose. Though this be padding yet there is method in it. And the method is to hide the clues.

Miss Marple's personality and behaviour are well suited to encouraging the kind of conversation that led Dora Bunner to indiscretion. So one might think that burying clues in froth is confined to the Marple novels. But this is not so.

In *The Clocks* (1963) two of the detectives visit Mr Bland, a local builder. Mr Bland is somewhat verbose and does most of the talking. There is a long conversation about gardening. Towards the end of the chapter Mr Bland talks about going on a cruise and how he likes travel but hasn't done much of it and has thought about living abroad, and so on. Mrs Bland chips in and says that although she also likes travel she would not want to live anywhere but in England, partly because her sister lives here. It is easy for the reader's attention to wander. But in just a couple of paragraphs two crucial nuggets of information have been slipped by the reader – nuggets that, if thought about carefully, can reveal the motive for murder.

Poirot is as much interested in encouraging people to talk as is Miss Marple. Sherlock Holmes focusses on minute clues such as a pile of dust, or a stain on the carpet: clues that others do not notice. Such physical details remain popular in modern TV series, from *CSI* to *Elementary* and *Sherlock*. Christie transformed such minute clues from the physical to the spoken, and in so doing makes them available to the reader. Poirot believes that there will usually be a word that gives a clue. In the case of Mr and Mrs Bland it is just two words.

In *The Clocks* Poirot plays a sedentary role, more Mycroft Holmes than Sherlock. It is not necessary, he says, to be a foxhound, but if he is to solve the case from his armchair, he needs a retriever. Colin Lamb is Poirot's retriever.

Six years previously Christie wrote a novel, *4.50 from Paddington* (1957), in which Miss Marple is almost completely sedentary. The retriever in that novel is the rather splendid Lucy Eyelesbarrow. She owes something to those young, feisty Christie heroines who populate many of the earlier novels, such as Tuppence, Lady 'Bundle' Brent and Lady Frances Derwent. But Lucy is a little different. Although she has a thirst for adventure and shows a lot of gumption and courage she is both more domestic, and more academic, than the classic Christie young women. Lucy is thirty-two years old. She has taken a First from Oxford in mathematics, has a brilliant mind and was confidently expected to take up an academic career. But she has, in addition to scholarly brilliance, what Christie sees as common sense. Perhaps thinking of her (second) husband, the academic archaeologist Max Mallowan, Christie writes that Lucy could see that academics are not well paid. And Lucy likes money, so she realised that the serious shortage of any kind of skilled domestic labour was an opportunity. She becomes a professional domestician. She hires herself out, for a couple of weeks or so at a time. Her niche is to take over managing a household to allow wives, for example, to go on trips abroad with their husbands.

4.50 from Paddington and *The Clocks* share another feature: they are the two Christie whodunnits in which the identity of the corpse is, for most of the novel, unknown.

This makes it difficult for the detectives, and the reader, to understand motive and to solve the crime. In the Miss Marple novel there is initially not even a corpse, only the report by Mrs McGillicuddy of witnessing a murder on a train through the window of another train. The body is eventually found after Miss Marple works out where it is likely to be. Miss Marple explains that she used a method described by Mark Twain in which a boy finds a horse by imagining himself as the horse and thinking about where he would go. Miss Marple imagines that she is the murderer on the train and thinks about where she would dump the body.

Christie's problem, with unidentified corpses, is how to ensure that the motive for the murder can be discovered. When Craddock asks Marple whether she thinks she knows who the murdered woman was, Marple replies somewhat enigmatically that in one sense she knows who she was but in another sense she does not know who she was. In *The Clocks*, when Colin Lamb says to Poirot that nobody knows who the dead man is, Poirot gives the almost identical reply. In the earlier novel it would be very difficult for the reader to have Miss Marple's insight – it is not well clued. In the later novel, however, Christie has solved the problem of how to provide a clue so that the reader too can know not *who* the victim is but at least who he *is*. The crucial clue is in the conversation with Mr and Mrs Bland.

The 'froth' – the padding – reduces the reader's attention because it is just a little dull. Sometimes Christie gives more life to the padding – more emotional tension – and then, whilst the reader's mind is focussed on the emotion, the clue quietly passes us by.

CHAPTER TWENTY-FOUR

Altering the tension

Lowering the reader's guard by manipulating emotion

Plot spoilers for: *After the Funeral.*

Poirot sits back in his chair with a coffee and watches and listens. The Abernethie family are disagreeing over who should inherit what, following the deaths of Richard Abernethie and his sister, Cora. The conversation becomes tense, the argument unpleasant. Who will get the green malachite table? Miss Gilchrist, who is not one of the family, intervenes in an attempt to placate the family members. But her intervention only irritates the family more. Miss Gilchrist is embarrassed. When someone mentions the wax flowers Miss Gilchrist remarks that the flowers looked good on the table. But nobody takes any notice of Miss Gilchrist, and the arguments continue. This scene is from *After the Funeral* (1953). Hidden within the dozen or so lines of dialogue is the single biggest clue in the novel – so well hidden that few readers will see it.

Christie uses a number of ways, cleverly intertwined, to hide the clue. First, to interpret it the reader must make use of information provided much earlier in the novel – an example of *sawing the clue in half* (chapter 18). Second, Miss Gilchrist witters on: an example of *buried in froth* (chapter 23). In addition Christie manipulates emotion so that Miss Gilchrist's intervention falls, as it were, below eye level: it is a brief lull in an otherwise tense scene. There are a number of stylish daubs to help achieve this effect: Miss Gilchrist's confusion, and the perfectly placed aside that nobody was taking any notice of her. And then, as soon as Miss Gilchrist has made her revealing statement Christie brings us back to the dispute over who should inherit the table.

Changing the tension is one way in which Christie makes use of emotion to manipulate the reader's attention. A bolder method is through humour, which she employs with considerable brio near the beginning of *A Murder Is Announced* (1950). Indeed she repeats the clue three times. The point is laboured, with amusing effect, that it was surprising to those gathered at the party that the central heating had been switched on. This is an important clue in the light of later events. Given its significance a lesser writer might have wanted to mention it, sotto voce, just the once. But Christie shouts it from the rooftops, which is what makes it funny, and, disguised as humour, the clue is likely to be lost in the laughter.

Although Christie uses humour to hide clues in only a few novels, most of her books are comic. Bargainnier argues that the kind of whodunnit that Christie writes, what are sometimes called 'cosy crime', are, from a formal point of view, *comedies*: the denouement provides a happy resolution to the various problems that have been put in the way of the 'detective hero'. Bargainnier writes:

> The central puzzle provides the usual complication, which the detective hero must remove; and its difficulty insures a typically comic engagement of the intellect. The whodunit's plot, full of deceptions, red herrings, clues real and fabricated, parallels the usually intricate plots of comedy, which often depend on mistaken motives, confusion, and dissembling.

Crime fiction is often talked about as a single genre. In many ways, however, the majority of Christie's books are closer to the English comic novel than to *noir* fiction. This is due not only to the final resolution but also to the humour throughout the novels. Christie writes in the tradition of the comedy of manners, mocking the foibles of the English, particularly of the upper classes. And although Hercule Poirot is serious in his actions, he is also a comic character: like a hairdresser in a comedy, is how Nurse Leatheran in *Murder in Mesopotamia* (1936) thinks of him. Some of the humour involves Poirot's often slightly odd English or the way he gets common phrases or proverbs just slightly wrong. Poirot's arrogance is also used to comic effect. When Inspector Morton (in *After the Funeral*) suggests that it would be rather boring to be always right Poirot simply replies that that is not what he has found.

Hastings, the narrator in some of the earlier books, is often the butt of the humour. In Christie's first published novel, *The Mysterious Affair at Styles*, Poirot says to Hastings that the two of them must be so intelligent that the murderer does not suspect them of being intelligent. Poirot then adds that Hastings will therefore be of help to him. Hastings tell us that this compliment pleased him.

Miss Marple is less an object of fun, but her observations can be quietly comic. By the 1960s, when Christie was in her seventies, Miss Marple is a little frail and although somewhat old-fashioned she has the wit to know it. In *The Mirror Crack'd from Side to Side* she is thinking, rather sadly, about how her village of St Mary Mead has changed over the years. She lists various reasons for this – reasons that people of her generation are likely to give: the two wars, the younger generation, women working outside the home, the Government. But she ends with a touch of self-mockery. Her sadness is a sign not that things are getting worse but that she is growing old.

British xenophobia is a frequent focus for Christie's mockery. In *Murder on the Orient Express* (1934) the American, Hector MacQueen, says of the valet, Masterman, that because he is British he has a poor opinion of Americans, and no opinion of people of any other nationality. And when, later in the book, Poirot is asked what Colonel Arbuthnot meant by saying that Miss Debenham is a *pukka sahib*, Poirot suggests that it means that like Arbuthnot, Miss Debenham's father and brothers were educated at an English public school.

British snobbery and the class system is another of Christie's targets. In *A Pocket Full of Rye* Miss Marple is thinking about Mrs Emmett, the bank manager's wife.

She did not really fit in to Miss Marple's village of St Mary Mead. On the one hand she was not one of the older ladies now in somewhat reduced circumstances; on the other hand she could not *of course* be friends with the wives of the tradesmen. The *of course* might at first be thought to reflect Christie's limited imagination, but the author's irony is made clear when she writes that snobbery had caused Mrs Emmett to be marooned on her own island of loneliness.

CHAPTER TWENTY-FIVE

The amiable murderer

Using the murderer's personality to befuddle the reader

Plot spoilers for: *The Seven Dials Mystery*; *The Man in the Brown Suit*; *Peril at End House*.

Some people find the idea distasteful that murder and its detection can be comic entertainment. There are brutish echoes of the Roman Empire's 'bread and circuses'. In horror films, or Nordic noir series, the perpetrators are usually cold psychopaths – their character magnifying the terror they produce. Such murderers are overtly evil oddballs often portrayed as loners outside society living in a snowy shack in some dark forest.

Christie, on the whole, writes feel-good 'cosy crime' stories. The gruesome details are kept to a minimum. The victims are often unpleasant, so one doesn't feel that bad when they die, or they are unknown to the reader so there is no emotional engagement at all. Christie's prose style is generally cheerful, and the dialogue funny. In striking contrast to more realistic crime dramas, Christie's murderers are often charming people, living normal lives, and at the centre of their social whirl.

In Christie's early thriller, *The Man in the Brown Suit* (1924), one of the characters remarks that in detective stories the villain is the most unlikely person and that many criminals are cheerful and fat. Sir Eustace Peddler's secretary is described as looking sinister – like a Borgia. You expect him to be a poisoner. Christie drops in a short discussion of Crippin, the famous real-life murderer, after a discussion about the secretary. We are being encouraged to associate the secretary with Crippin. Christie is manipulating the reader's subconscious.

Sir Eustace – a cheerful, fat businessman – finds it amusing that his secretary looks like a murderer. He goes on to vouch for the secretary's character and adds that no murderer who had any self-respect would look so much like a murderer.

Sir Eustace Peddler is charming, immensely rich, witty and clever. In Jane Austen terms he 'must be in want of a wife'. Sir Eustace may not be as young as the normal dashing romantic hero, nor as handsome, but the reader knows life with him would always be fun. The dictionary defines *amiable* as 'possessing that friendly disposition which causes one to be liked. Having pleasing qualities'. Sir Eustace is very amiable. At the big reveal the feisty young Christie heroine confronts Sir Eustace with being the criminal mastermind. Without any rancour Sir Eustace freely admits everything, and then proposes! He knows that women cannot testify against husbands and he feels that marriage would be the pleasantest solution, rather than killing her, as would happen in a James Bond plot. Sir Eustace is one of very few Christie criminals who gets away with murder. Perhaps he charmed Christie as much as he charms the reader.

In many of Christie's adventure stories the central characters are a young couple in love who solve a crime together. Like all good comedies the books end with matrimony. The names of the young people may change but the pattern is the same. The first of these young people were Tommy and Tuppence Beresford in *The Secret Adversary* (1922). Tuppence was Agatha's alter ego, and Tommy, an amiable young man, probably based loosely on Archie – Agatha's first husband.

The Christies had survived the First World War, and despite the Depression they were full of enthusiasm and energy. Archie was dashing, handsome and charming. He persuaded Agatha to break off an engagement to another man and to marry him instead. Archie was an early airplane pilot, qualifying in 1912. He joined the Royal Flying Corps in the war, and was distinguished for bravery (DSO and CMG). He had difficulty readjusting to post-war life. There are several characters in Christie novels who are dashing, handsome young men with a good war record, particularly in her books written after the Second World War.

One example is David Hunter in *Taken at the Flood* (1948) who had been a commando, and steals the girl in the story from the bovine farmer. Hunter knows he is attractive to women, and plays on his charm. A kind of Lord Byron. He is a complex mix of good and ill woven together, melded in the furnace of a terrible war. It is an irony that Hunter spends most of the book defending himself for a murder he did not commit, whilst continuing to be secretly wicked with relish.

The Seven Dials Mystery (1929) looks to be another adventure in the same mould as *The Secret Adversary*. It begins with Jimmy Thesiger, described as an amiable youth rushing down the stairs. He collides with the butler in the hall and apologises, showing his impeccable good breeding. Set in Chimneys, the English ancestral home of Lord Caterham, this is a classic country-house Christie. A party of Bright Young Things with silly nicknames like 'Pongo', 'Bundle' and 'Socks' is in full swing, with boating on the lake and tea on the lawn. It is all giggles and innocent japes. These are thoughtless wealthy young people. The reader's sympathy is entirely with the butler, who serves them stoically. When one of the young men is found dead the mood suddenly changes from Brideshead to Chimneys revisited.

Jimmy Thesiger sets out to find the murderer, aided by Lorraine Wade. Lorraine is the classic Christie heroine: blonde, beautiful with cornflower-blue eyes. Jimmy Thesiger loves her. All readers adore young innocent people in love and fired up with a good cause. There is, unusually, another young couple, Lady Brent and Bill Eversleigh, who join forces with Thesiger and Wade. Brent and Eversleigh helped Superintendent Battle in the earlier novel, *The Secret of Chimneys*, so the reader knows they are good eggs. Bill was friends with the murdered young man, and acquainted with Jimmy Thesiger, so Thesiger must also be a good egg, by association.

Christie wrote *The Seven Dials Mystery* shortly after she had felt forced to acquiesce to Archie Christie's request for a divorce. Perhaps this is why two of the four Young Adventurers, the ones most like Archie and his new love, come to a very bad end indeed. The amiable youth turns out to be a depraved and callous criminal.

Christie uses the idea of the amiable murderer to good effect in several of her whodunnits. In *Peril at End House* (1932) Nick Buckley not only charms Poirot (Hastings suggests that Poirot has fallen in love); she charms the reader as well. We feel sorry for her and want to protect her from harm. But, it turns out, she is an amiable murderer: a black widow spider welcoming you into her web.

Do not take home the message that all of Christie's murderers are amiable. Some, from the start, are unpleasant; others are just dull. Neither are all the amiable characters murderers: some are victims, the majority innocent bystanders. Sometimes Christie deceives us with a bluff, sometimes with a double bluff and sometimes with no bluff at all. And sometimes it is the detective who deceives us.

CHAPTER TWENTY-SIX

The deceptive detective

Using the detective's authority to bamboozle

Plot spoilers for: *The Mysterious Affair at Styles*; *The Clocks*.

Suspects, in a whodunnit, rarely tell the detective the whole truth. Frequently they lie in order to deceive. Poirot thinks that it is his job to distinguish harmless lies from important lies (*Hercule Poirot's Christmas*). But in *Dead Man's Folly* we are told that Poirot himself can lie better than anyone else.

The purpose of the detectives' deceptions may be to gull another character, but by doing so they can also mislead the reader. Sometimes the detectives are themselves mistaken. Even the smartest detectives can be misled by red herrings – or red kippers, as Poirot is wont to call them. It all adds to the excitement of the plot.

For most readers there is an assumption that the detectives and the police are decent, and reliable. Christie plays with this assumption. She may use the authority of the detectives to slip a false deduction into the reader's mind. There are three ways that trust in such authority can be misplaced: the detective may simply be wrong; a villain may be disguised as a respected law-enforcement officer; and, just occasionally in a Christie novel, a real policeman or detective is the murderer. Gaston Leroux, one of Christie's inspirations, shocked readers in *The Mystery of the Yellow Room* (1907) with his criminal police inspector.

In *The Mysterious Affair at Styles* (1920) Mr Inglethorpe is the obvious suspect. Inglethorpe is a bit too obvious. Then Poirot appears to prove that he is not the murderer. Poirot says to Hastings (and of course also to the reader) that Mr Inglethorpe cannot be the murderer. Poirot, on this occasion, is wrong.

In *Towards Zero* (1944) the police are searching a house for clues after Lady Tressilian has been murdered in her bed. Superintendent Battle, Inspector Leach and PC Jones decide to start methodically at the top of the house and work their way down. When Jones says that he hasn't searched the box room, Battle tells him not to bother – the dust, he says, shows that no one has been in the room in a long while. Clearly the police had resource issues even in 1944. The local PC and most readers trust the experience and judgement of the superintendent from Scotland Yard. So we clump downstairs together with the police, and miss the clue in the dusty lumber-room that might save an innocent person from the hangman's noose.

It is a useful compass for readers of Christie novels that the truth is always the opposite of Hastings' opinions. If Hastings is pointing north, head south. Whenever Hastings assures Poirot that someone is a 'good egg' they will turn out to be a bounder or a cad, or worse. Poirot sometimes deceives Hastings intentionally. In *The Big Four* (1927) Poirot says to Hastings that he may have to involve his twin brother, Achille, in the case. Christie enjoys a nod to Sherlock Holmes and his brother, Mycroft, when Poirot tells Hastings that all detectives have a brilliant but lazy brother. When Hastings asks Poirot whether Achille looks like him Poirot answers that there are similarities but that Achille is not as handsome, and has no moustache.

Several months after Hercule Poirot has been assassinated, Hastings and Achille Poirot are captured by the Big Four. They are taken to the Big Four's world domination control centre to be killed, prefiguring all the *James Bond* stories by nearly thirty years. Hastings is upset when he realises that Poirot has been deceiving him but Poirot placates him sweetly. It was necessary to deceive the 'baddies' and Hastings is such a lovely and honest person that he could only deceive if he himself was deceived.

In *The Mirror Crack'd from Side to Side* (1962), the reader's perspective is subtly misdirected when Miss Marple speculates on the social standing of Marina Gregg's killer. In this case Miss Marple herself is mistaken.

In *The Clocks* (1963) Inspector Hardcastle and Colin Lamb go from door to door down a street interviewing the neighbours after a murder. They question the rather dodgy builder, Mr Bland. Inspector Hardcastle, however, is not interested in a crooked builder. He might poison his wife to get her money, he suggests, but that is not the type of murderer in this case. Instead of worrying about Mr Bland, he tells Lamb, they should get on with solving the murder in hand. We are likely to be as impatient as

Inspector Hardcastle and to dismiss Bland the builder from our minds in order to get on with finding the real killer.

Disguise is one of the major ways in which characters can deceive both readers and the police. But the detectives themselves may sometimes be in disguise. In the Sherlock Holmes story, *The Man with the Twisted Lip*, even the observant Dr Watson walks straight past a bent and wrinkled old man in an opium den without recognising his friend. Hercule Poirot, on one occasion, as we have seen, disguises himself as his fictional twin brother, Achille, fooling his friend Hastings. Generally, though, both Poirot and Miss Marple avoid such dressing-up. In *Mrs McGinty's Dead* (1952) Superintendent Spence asks Poirot if he will go incognito to investigate. Poirot seems offended and says in no uncertain terms that he will go as Hercule Poirot.

This boast, however, is itself deceptive because Poirot's appearance and manner *are* a disguise. It is a long-running joke between author and reader that Poirot plays up his 'foreign' ways. In *Three Act Tragedy* (1934) Poirot admits this. He says that he is perfectly able to speak impeccable English but that speaking like a foreigner leads people – the English in particular – to despise him. He also admits to boasting in order that the English will think less of him. In these ways people underestimate him and are not so careful in what they say to him.

Christie uses the fact that Poirot is so obviously 'foreign' to lampoon British prejudice. Indeed Poirot comes in for such continual verbal abuse that one wonders why he stays in England at all. For example, in *Taken at the Flood* (1948) Poirot is attempting to sit in the lounge bar of a pub. The widow of Canon Leadbetter, who is nearly eighty years old and supposedly full of Christian charity, says to Poirot that the English fought the war so that foreigners could go back to where they came from, and stay there! In the same novel, Major Porter looks at Poirot, sees his shiny shoes, trousers, coat and moustache, and remarks that even in his club he is not free from foreigners.

Poirot seems generally to be unaffected by insults and prejudice, but in *Mrs McGinty's Dead* (1952), he winces with pain when he hears himself described as French and as looking like a hairdresser. It is not clear whether he is upset by being mistaken for a Frenchman, or a hairdresser, or both. Near the end of the book Poirot reveals himself not as the man inviting ridicule but as the hunter closing in on his target.

Unlike Poirot, who has to work hard to get his shiny patent-leather shoes inside the door, Miss Marple's upbringing in a cathedral close gives her immediate acceptance into all circles of English society. Marple witters on, knitting and listening to gossip in the corners of some of the best country-house drawing rooms. Her greatest strength is that she is equally at home amongst the upper classes, or in a shabby vicarage armchair, or at a Women's Institute meeting in the draughty village hall. She is a chameleon, camouflaged, but with her beady eyes and ears always alert, and snapping up titbits of clues, like juicy flies. She is an iron fist in an angora mitten of her own design. She plays up the infirmities of age. Her dithery, incomprehensible stories about people living in St Mary Mead lull suspects into thinking she is a harmless old woman with early cognitive decline, and she is often pitied. Like Poirot, Marple knows that she is in disguise and admits (in *Nemesis*, 1971) that she pretends to be a scatty old woman as a camouflage. She makes it clear in *The Body in the Library* (1942) that underneath the camouflage there is a tough, sceptical mind that never believes anyone.

Most of the characters underestimate Miss Marple, but not Inspector Craddock in *A Murder Is Announced* (1950), who considers her as a rattlesnake; and not Gina in *They Do It with Mirrors* (1952), who calls her a wicked old woman.

CHAPTER TWENTY-SEVEN

The double bluff

Fooling those readers who think they know the author
and the genre

Plot spoilers for: *Taken at the Flood*.

The origin of the word 'bluff' meaning to deceive or hoodwink is itself appropriately obscure. According to the Oxford English Dictionary a *bluff* was a protective blinker for a horse and *to bluff* came to mean to blindfold. From there the sense became more metaphorical and developed its modern meaning by way of the card game poker.

A double bluff is a paradox: it is both a bluff and not a bluff. A standard definition of double bluff is 'a statement meant to seem to be a bluff but in fact genuine'. But the double bluff is also intended to deceive and is therefore also a bluff, of a kind.

The wonderful elderly character Lady Matilda Cleckheaton asserts in *Passenger to Frankfurt* (1970) that in life, as in knitting, there is a limited number of patterns. Lady Matilda is an amalgam of Ariadne Oliver and Miss

Marple with a dash of Oscar Wilde's Lady Bracknell. Her philosophy is that being interesting is more important than being good-looking. She modestly explains how she solved the mystery, exactly as Miss Marple would have done. As readers we can try and take a leaf out of Lady Matilda's book and look for the patterns in how Christie sets her puzzles. We might come to believe, based on one or two examples, that if the victim, in what looks like an attempted murder, survives then it was not a genuine attempt. Is this a pattern – one of Christie's bluffs? Christie, however, is quite capable of turning the patterns inside out. We might think that she is knitting a cardigan but it turns out to be a sock, or a red herring. In writing her novels she might set a trail of bluffs and then cast off a double bluff to keep you guessing. We should not have liked to play Christie at poker, or bridge. Just when we think we know her she writes a novel in which the attempted murder really was a murder gone wrong.

Christie bluffs and double bluffs continually, either in a small way (a chance remark of one of the characters that leads us astray), or as a serious misdirection, or as the principal structure of a plot. An example of the chance remark is when Sergeant Fletcher, in *A Murder Is Announced* (1950), realising that a door was mysteriously oiled, muses to himself that one of the characters cannot be the murderer as he would not have had to use the door. We immediately think that that character is all the more suspicious. But, in fact, Fletcher is right. We have been misled by the simplest of double bluffs.

An example of a more substantial double bluff involves the classic whodunnit trope of the defaced corpse. If a corpse is defaced we immediately think that this is not a corpse of the person it appears to be (chapter 9). Then, from time to time, there is a defaced corpse whose identity *is* who it is thought to be: a double bluff. Christie uses many of the expectations of the genre to cast her double bluffs. She even creates a double, double bluff, a kind of triple bluff.

In *Taken at the Flood* (1948), the mysterious Enoch Arden is found murdered in his room in a local pub. Arden had been blackmailing David Hunter. The police arrest Hunter for Arden's murder but his meticulously watertight alibi gets him released. Knowing Christie, we think that only murderers require a good alibi, so Hunter must be guilty. Innocent people have no need of alibis, nor do they know when one is required. We spend the whole novel trying to find a chink in his story. The double bluff is that he did create a false alibi but did not murder Enoch Arden. We find out, in the end, that Arden's death was not even murder: a triple bluff.

We have seen that in several of Christie's novels the central plot is a bluff because she breaks the unwritten rules of the whodunnit genre. In some novels a central part of the plot is a double bluff. There are several novels in which the murderer disguises himself as someone else whilst committing the murder. This is a common bluff in crime novels in general. In one novel, however, Christie's murderer disguises himself as... himself: a double bluff.

In all these examples we are being manipulated to view the puzzle from the perspective of the bluff, not of the double bluff – just one example of how Christie promotes a deceptive perspective.

CHAPTER TWENTY-EIGHT

The deceptive perspective

Concealing the solution by providing a misleading
point of view

Plot spoilers for: *The Sittaford Mystery*; *After the Funeral*.

Christie likes to fool us into looking at the case the
wrong way up. In order to get the solution we have
to change perspective, and, if we are successful, in a flash
all is clear. Puzzles that give us that 'eureka' moment – the
sudden 'aha' – are particularly satisfying. Christie's use
of the deceptive perspective is one of her most enjoyable
deceits.

   Christie sometimes used plot to provide the misleading
perspective; for example, the apparent victim is not the
intended victim – an example of a bluff. Sometimes she
used dialogue. Often plot and dialogue work together.
Like a conjuror she forces on the reader the deceiving
point of view. There is a good example in *Three Act
Tragedy* (1935). There have been two murders. One of the
characters takes us through a kind of Socratic dialogue.
Did the same person kill the two people? Yes. Was the

second person killed because he knew who had murdered the first person? Yes. So it is the first murder on which we must concentrate – which will tell us the main motive. Of course.

This argument rehearses a frequently used method to increase the body count in a crime novel. A murder is committed for a standard reason, such as gain. One or more subsequent murders are then committed to conceal the identity of the murderer. Christie used this expectation to deceive. In *Three Act Tragedy* it is the second murder that is key. The first murder is a blind. Christie, however, does not rely on plot alone to deceive: the dialogue above reinforces the false perspective.

In other novels Christie uses a false perspective to conceal a clue. Near the beginning of *The Sittaford Mystery* (1931) there is a 'table-turning' – a séance – which provides a brilliant dramatic first act to the novel. At the séance the spirit gives the message to the effect that one of the characters has been murdered. It turns out that at about the time of the séance that character was indeed murdered. The whole scene, if considered in the right way, can lead the reader to the solution, as we have seen in an earlier chapter (chapter 14). Christie tackles this head-on. Emily Trefusis, one of Christie's young women detectives, says that we cannot ignore the séance. She is voicing exactly what many readers will have been thinking. She goes on to outline three explanations for the message: first that it was supernatural, second that someone spelt out the message deliberately and third that someone spelt out the message accidentally – an unconscious piece of self-revelation. She, like any reader of Christie, dismisses the supernatural. She rapidly discounts the second explanation, saying that there is no possible reason. She then elaborates the idea of the unconscious and concludes that two people are involved: one person who was at the séance, and an accomplice who was committing the murder six miles away. In the next chapter one of the people at the séance is having tea with the murdered man's sister – a person with motive and opportunity to murder. The reader can easily become focussed on this third explanation and almost unconsciously dismiss the second, much more likely explanation.

Thirty years later, in *The Mirror Crack'd from Side to Side* (1962), Christie used the same technique but with more subtlety – more elegance. Miss Marple is talking to her general practitioner, Dr Haydock. She is wondering why no one has admitted to seeing someone put the pills into the drink that killed Heather Badcock. Miss Marple suggests three possible reasons. The first is that someone noticed but did not realise that what they saw was important. The second is that the murderer picked up Heather Badcock's glass and openly added the poison but that anyone who did see would assume that the glass belonged to the murderer and that they were adding their own medication.

The doctor quickly sums up Miss Marple's first two reasons: the first assumes an idiot, the second a risk-taker. What is Miss Marple's third reason? And so the reader has almost dismissed possibilities one and two and focusses on possibility three – which is that someone did see and is blackmailing the murderer. The next chapter is about a possible blackmailer.

In both these examples, Christie has, perhaps intuitively, made use of a robust finding in psychological research: that when given a list, we tend to remember best the items at the beginning and end of the list. Items in the middle are the most easily forgotten, and ignored.

In *After the Funeral* (1953), and in contrast with the examples given above, Christie provides the misleading perspective *before* giving the clue. At the beginning of the book the wealthy Richard Abernethie has died. At the gathering after his funeral Cora suggests that Richard was murdered. Cora is found murdered the following day. Much later in the book Poirot asks Richard's sister-in-law, Helen, who, of those who had been at the gathering, had known Cora best. And when it seems that Helen herself knew her as well as anyone Poirot asks her why she thinks Cora had said what she did. This whole discussion is a significant clue, but the clue has nothing to do with who knew Cora best, nor what she meant by what she had said. The clue is that no one knew Cora very well at all. Few readers will pick this up because Poirot has focussed our attention elsewhere.

Just occasionally Christie will use perspective to help rather than hinder the reader in solving the puzzle. In *They Do It with Mirrors* (1952) there is a conversation between Inspector Curry and Alex Restarick about stage sets and what is behind them, and whether they are real or not.

At the end of the conversation Restarick is struck by a sudden thought. He says that the inspector has just made a penetrating remark. This is Christie's way of letting us know that the conversation is significant in some way. As so often she is teasing the reader, laying down the gauntlet, as it were: 'I'm giving you a clue, but I challenge you to make sense of it.' But it is a clue. It provides a perspective that could help. If the reader thinks of the murder as *staged* then what is crucial is what had gone on *behind the scenes*.

Alex Restarick is echoing Poirot from a much earlier novel. In *Murder on the Orient Express* (1934) Poirot says that a remark made by his friend Monsieur Bouc is profound. In that novel Christie has to keep the reader from looking in the right direction. She does this not with a misleading point of view but by constantly posing a misleading question: the question as decoy.

CHAPTER TWENTY-NINE

The question as decoy

Posing a question that leads readers astray

Plot spoilers for: *A Murder Is Announced*; *Murder on the Orient Express*.

Christie could use a well-posed question to start every hare running in different directions. By asking the wrong questions, Christie sets the reader down the wrong path – a path that, as in a well-planned maze, leads to a cul-de-sac, or to an interesting red herring. Questions asked, particularly by characters of authority, often conceal the crooked path to the correct solution. They divert our gaze, like a conjuror's trick, to a glittering false hypothesis, which may then explode in a puff of smoke.

Perhaps the best-known question in English literature is: 'To be or not to be?'

Hamlet's father has died. The key questions are was he murdered, and if so, by whom. Hamlet, however, spends the whole play distracted by the question he poses himself and musing on melancholic metaphysics, rather than focussing on solving his father's untimely death. If only

Hercule Poirot had been staying for a long weekend at Elsinore things might have turned out very differently.

In the classic *A Murder Is Announced* (1950), the trusted Miss Marple says to the chief constable that he must find out who wanted to kill Miss Blacklock. A few pages later Inspector Craddock says to his superior that someone attempted to kill Miss Blacklock. He then asks why. We obediently start trying to answer the question, *why*? rather than doubting the premiss on which it is based.

Murder on the Orient Express (1934) is such a famous, groundbreaking whodunnit that it is hard to imagine reading it in ignorance of the solution. The daring nature of the plot posed Christie with the major problem of how to be fair in providing clues without making the solution too obvious. One of her techniques was to pose the wrong questions.

The victim, the suspects and Poirot are confined to one carriage on a train that is stuck in deep snow in the middle of what was then Yugoslavia. Someone in the carriage was murdered by an odd assortment of twelve different stab wounds. Poirot's job is to find the murderer before the train moves on. There are a large number of suspects. The question that Christie aims to keep uppermost in our mind is: which of them (is the murderer)? The question is even used as a chapter title. This decoy question is hammered into our brain so deeply, again and again, that we focus on trying to find the clues that can point us to one of the suspects more than to the others. This focus on one murderer is further strengthened when Poirot wonders whether, despite the victim having so many wounds, we can be sure that more than one person had stabbed him. What reasons could there be, other than more than one killer, for the multiple wounds? Readers are being encouraged – and misdirected – to come up with clever reasons for assuming a single murderer.

The story of the novel's origins is impressive and inspiring. In December 1931 Agatha Christie travelled alone on the Orient Express from Stamboul (Istanbul) to London. At about 3am on the first night of the journey the train stopped. The line was flooded. In a letter to her (second) husband, Max Mallowan, Christie described some of her fellow passengers, including a Hungarian minister, a Danish missionary and a director of the Wagon Lits company. Christie was stranded for two days on a train hit by floods and snow. Many of us would have been frustrated and angry. Christie amused herself by exercising her imagination. She spent her time weaving her disparate fellow travellers (or stationary companions) into one of the most famous whodunnits ever written. From adversity she created the setting and many of the characters of *Murder on the Orient Express* – she created something rich and strange. To a writer of Christie's stature no experience, however inconvenient, is wasted. The two of us try to learn from Christie every time the train to London is delayed. Rather than fuming, we attempt to tell ourselves a story that links our fellow travellers together.

CHAPTER THIRTY

Shifting the gaze

Diverting the reader's focus whilst slipping in the clue

Plot spoilers for: *Death on the Nile.*

A good whodunnit writer, as we have suggested several times, is something of a stage magician. Both wish to entertain. Both hoodwink their audience to achieve their effects. Both have to take their audience along with them on the journey to get to the surprise at the end. Stage magicians have the additional advantage that they can use light and sound to manipulate the audience. Bright spotlights and the swift movements of assistants are used to direct our gaze; dark areas of the stage can conceal. A loud drum roll might startle and excite. All aid the legerdemain performance. These techniques go back at least to Mesmer in the late eighteenth century, who is credited with founding modern hypnotherapy.

Christie had magic at her fingertips, using her typewriter to create an imaginary but vivid world. She distracts our gaze using her characters, their movements, their conversations and their emotions so that the clues slip deftly by without our noting them. We have already seen how our attention wanders when Christie distracts us with froth, and how our attention is grabbed by emotion when she varies the tension.

Sometimes she shifts our gaze away from the clue with just a simple statement or two. In *The Mirror Crack'd from Side to Side* (1962) Marina takes a sip of coffee, says it tastes bitter and drinks no more. Marina's friends think that she is being rather hysterical but the coffee is sent for analysis and it is found to have contained arsenic. One of the characters comments that Marina was therefore right about the coffee tasting bitter. Marina's husband says that actually arsenic has no taste but that Marina's instinct was right. Marina wasn't being hysterical after all. The important clue here is that arsenic has no taste – Marina was lying about the taste. But it is easy for us to miss this and to accept without thinking that she has somehow known by intuition that the coffee was poisoned.

Sometimes Christie distracts us not with simplicity but with complexity. In *Hickory Dickory Dock* (1955) there are so many students in the boarding houses in Hickory Road that we are bewildered by the bustle and crowds.

Death on the Nile (1937) is one of the best-clued Christies (chapter 7). Yet it is difficult to withstand the barrage of ways in which Christie subverts our reasoning. Jackie, who is in love with Simon, has been stalking Simon and his wife, Linnet, whilst they are on holiday in Egypt. Jackie gets a malicious pleasure from seeing Linnet upset. We empathise with both sides. In one of the key scenes there is so much going on that it is difficult to know where to look. The scene, which takes place just before Linnet's murder, involves a spectacular row between Simon and Jackie. Two other people are present. Christie well expresses the different actions and feelings of the four characters. Jackie is angry, Simon full of regret. Cornelia and Jim are squirming with embarrassment. Then Jackie shoots at Simon. He is wounded. Help is sought. Jackie tries to throw herself overboard. All is panic, anxiety and concern. There are, in fact, several clues in this scene but in the mayhem they are kicked under the sofa with the pistol. The whirling action sweeps us away down the Nile. The excitement distracts us, and the clues float silently by. In scenes like this we need to focus on the darkest corner of the stage rather than let our gaze be dazzled by the spotlight.

Christie is rarely taken seriously as a writer. Edmund Wilson wrote in 1945 that Christie's writing is of a mawkishness and banality that he found literally impossible to read. Millions throughout the world would disagree. The novelist Robert Graves was a friend of Max Mallowan. They were both Oxford classicists. Graves became a friend of Mrs Mallowan – Agatha Christie. Graves dedicated his novel *The Golden Fleece* to Agatha and Max. However, he was patronising about Christie as a writer and described her English as schoolgirlish. This overweening arrogance may explain Christie's somewhat teasing reciprocal dedication to Graves in *Towards Zero* (1944), in which she asks him to withhold his critical faculties.

It is easy to underestimate Christie's apparently simple, direct and highly readable style. Her clarity, however, needs to be celebrated, not pilloried. The scene from *Death on the Nile* mentioned above is so vivid and interesting that we are swept up in the action. Christie has that power to make us turn the pages, not wanting to stop until we get to the end. In literary circles her popular appeal has been her downfall: few academics take Christie, or indeed the whole whodunnit genre, seriously as classic literary texts. Too low-brow? Loathe her or like her, her success, continuing popularity and power to stimulate creative responses require explanation.

CHAPTER THIRTY-ONE

Disappearing in a puff of smoke

Providing a false explanation immediately after the clue

No plot spoilers.

There are, almost always, several possible explanations for any single observation. One reason may be correct, another false. Sometimes the false explanation is given out of ignorance; sometimes it is offered in the knowledge that it is false, perhaps from kindness – a white lie – or perhaps for darker reasons.

Christie sometimes uses false explanations for comic effect, and to make readers feel smug. We get a pleasure when there is a false explanation that we are clever enough to see through. Part of the enduring appeal of loveable Arthur Hastings, and of Dr Watson before him, is that we are not fooled as they are. Hastings is often the comic fall guy.

In *Murder in Mesopotamia* (1936) the narrator is not Hastings but Nurse Leatheran. When Mrs Louise Leidner – a femme fatale – is being charming to Joseph Mercardo, Leatheran tells us that she wants to let Mrs Leidner know that her innocent behaviour might make Mercardo's wife jealous. Nurse Leatheran is giving a kindly but false explanation for Mrs Leidner's behaviour that we do *not* fall for. The nurse is a character who always sees the best in people. We smile to ourselves, knowing exactly what sort of woman Louise Leidner really is. But there are explanations in the novel that we may well fall for.

Leatheran has been employed to look after the beautiful Mrs Leidner. Louise Leidner, however, is an able-bodied woman in her late thirties. The fact that she has a nurse to look after her while on an archaeological dig is an important clue. But it is explained away by several of the others at the dig so that the reader is unlikely to see that it is a clue. The explanations are that Louise is given to 'nerves', or, less sympathetically, that she enjoys the attention. These explanations seem completely reasonable in the light of her character. Louise Leidner has to be the centre of everyone's attention. The harassed but devoted Dr Leidner – Louise's husband – probably had to draft in a competent nurse to give the archaeologists at the dig a breather from Louise's incessant demands, and also time to get on with the work of digging and cataloguing the finds. As a reader you stop thinking about Nurse Leatheran, and simply accept her as narrator.

In *A Murder Is Announced* (1950) two false explanations are given in rapid succession immediately after an important clue. The clue appears and disappears all within a couple of sentences. One of the main characters, Miss Blacklock, always wears a close-fitting necklace of pearls. In one scene the necklace breaks. Miss Blacklock is quite extraordinarily upset. She rushes from the room, her hand to her throat. Phillipa suggests that the reason why Miss Blacklock is upset might be because the pearls had been a present from someone special. Inspector Craddock wonders whether the pearls might have been real – sufficiently valuable to provide a motive to try and kill Miss Blacklock. Neither of these explanations is correct, nor, if thought about carefully, are they convincing, but they can be sufficient for the important clue to disappear from the reader's mind before it is even noticed.

Cat Amongst the Pigeons (1959) is set in the best girls' boarding school in England. It is the beginning of the academic year. Miss Bulstrode, the headmistress, and Miss Chadwick, the deputy head, are discussing the new French mistress, Mademoiselle Blanche. Miss Chadwick considers her sly. Miss Bulstrode says that she is not a good teacher despite having had good references. After the first murder the police interview Mademoiselle Blanche. Their verdict is that, like all French people, she is touchy. Miss Chadwick and the policeman independently offer xenophobic generalisations to explain away Mademoiselle Blanche's behaviour and her disappointing abilities as a teacher. Miss Bulstrode, one of the best headteachers in England, accepts Miss Chadwick's explanation rather than trusting her own observations. The reader has already been told that Miss Bulstrode is weary and thinking of retirement. It is all too easy for us, as readers, to follow Miss Bulstrode's lead and to miss completely the important clue.

In the Second World War thriller *N or M* (1941), there is a dramatic scene when a Polish refugee kidnaps a toddler, Betty Sprot. A group of local notables, including

Commander Haydock, Major Bletchley and Betty's mother, follow this refugee onto the cliff top to plead for Betty's safe return. The refugee holds the baby close to her so that Commander Haydock cannot risk shooting because he might hit Betty. And then Betty's mother shoots the refugee dead in the head. Betty is unharmed. Commander Haydock calls it a miracle – perhaps a mother's instinct. It is easy for us to accept Commander Haydock's explanation. If we do, we miss two significant clues.

N or M is a spy thriller, and, because there is a lot of incidental detail, it is an interesting historical document of Britain at war. Christie's American editors at first rejected the book (in 1940) because they thought that such a clearly anti-Nazi novel might upset a significant portion of their readers. Christie had seen the novel as her contribution to the war effort.

N or M got Christie into exceedingly hot water at home in Britain. One of the minor characters in the book is called Major Bletchley. This must have made some hearts miss a beat in the War Office. Bletchley Park was the top-secret British code-breaking establishment during the war. When the book was published with mentions of Bletchley and code-cracking, MI5 were concerned there had been a serious breach of security. Their concern was all the greater because Professor Sir Alfred Dillwyn Knox (known as Dilly Knox), who was one of the lead code breakers at Bletchley Park, was also a personal friend of Christie and her husband Max Mallowan. MI5 officers were sent to question Knox. Knox invited Christie to visit his house. Over tea and scones Knox asked Christie why she had chosen the name Bletchley for a character in her new book. Christie replied that it was an act of revenge: she had been delayed at Bletchley on a train from Oxford to London.

Hard to believe? Possibly a false explanation after the clue she had given about activities at Bletchley? Bletchley railway station was on the line from Oxford to Cambridge but not on the line from Oxford to London. Besides Major Bletchley is hardly unlovable: he is just a minor character. As an aside, Dilly Knox was brother to Ronald Knox, whom we met in chapter 1 as the author of the Ten Commandments of Detective Fiction.

After *N or M*, for the rest of the war, Christie steered well away from thrillers with contemporary political references. She resumed cosy crime, writing some excellent whodunnits such as *Evil Under the Sun*, *The Body in the Library* and *Five Little Pigs*, but with no references to the war whatsoever. It was only in 1948 that Christie published her exceedingly bitter book *Taken at the Flood*, set contemporaneously in post-war England. It is an outpouring of grief following the death of her son-in-law, killed in action in 1944 (chapter 5).

CHAPTER THIRTY-TWO

Double-dealing

Giving a clue and a misdirection together in the same
package

Plot spoilers for: *Crooked House.*

M ost Christie clues come with a misdirection. Usually
the misdirection is just after the clue. Sometimes it
is in the set-up before the clue. Just occasionally Christie
pulls off one of her most devilish deceits: the clue and the
misdirection are one and the same. She helps and hinders
in the same breath. That breath may be an extended
conversation as in *Crooked House* (1949), or a single
sentence as in *Sleeping Murder* (1976).

In *Crooked House* there is a long discussion between
Charles Hayward, the romantic lead, and his father, Sir
Arthur Hayward, who is a senior policeman (chapter 22).
Charles asks his father what in his experience murderers
are like. Sir Arthur's answer leads Charles to consider
which of the suspects are morally immature. It also
suggests that a child could kill. Two ways of responding to
the argument: one a clue, the other a misdirection.

Sleeping Murder, although the last of Christie's novels to be published, had been written twenty-five or so years earlier (chapter 10). The story is about the disappearance, possibly the murder, of Helen, twenty years ago. One piece of evidence that Helen was not murdered – that she ran away – is a postcard that she apparently sent from abroad. The postcard is examined by a handwriting expert together with a known sample of Helen's handwriting. Gwenda believes that Helen was murdered, so when the report from the handwriting expert arrives she predicts that it will show that the postcard was not written by Helen. Giles reads the report and tells her that it was. In just two words Christie gives both a misdirection and the most significant clue in the book. Readers will have assumed that Helen had been murdered – this is an Agatha Christie novel, after all. But now the whole assumption of the novel is brought into question: is Helen still alive? Many readers will follow Gwenda and Giles down this cul-de-sac. But those readers who refuse the misdirection can immediately identify the murderer. Miss Marple, of course, picks up the clue. Towards the end of the book she tells Giles his mistake: he believed what people told him – a dangerous thing to do. She hasn't believed people for a very long time.

Miss Marple is something of a double dealer herself, hiding her sharp intelligence under a cloak of fluttering and dithering (chapter 26). But it is not all conscious disguise. Her personality is one of contrasts and contradictions. On the one hand she is cold and unbending; on the other hand she is kind and fun.

The steely, tough side to Miss Marple is rooted in her Victorian upbringing – brought up to do her duty. On one occasion she says that we should not avoid danger, and indeed she can show a great deal of courage – not least when she attacks the murderer, saving Gwenda's life, at the end of *Sleeping Murder*. But the toughness can spill over into callousness. She is hardly troubled at all when, in *A Murder Is Announced* (1950), she causes the death of Dora Bunner by encouraging Dora to talk in a public place. She admits that the conversation did lead directly to Dora's death but goes on to suggest that Dora would have been murdered at some point anyway. This really is letting herself off the hook. We get a good picture of her emotional priorities at the end of *A Pocket Full of Rye* (1953). She looks at a photo of the murdered Gladys – who had been her maid, and whose murder she has just solved. She is moved to a few tears of pity. She then feels anger at the murderer but almost immediately her overwhelming emotion is of triumph – the triumph that a palaeontologist might feel on managing to reconstruct an extinct animal from a bone fragment. The Assistant Commissioner of Scotland Yard describes her as ruthless and the Home Secretary says that she is the most frightening woman he has met.

Miss Marple's Victorian upbringing might also account for her discomfort when talking about pregnancy, and her blushes when discussing the relationship between an elderly man and a young woman. Sex might embarrass her, but she is not naïve. On holiday in the Caribbean (*A Caribbean Mystery*, 1964) she starts thinking about sex. She has no desire to talk or write about sex, we are told, but she knew all about sex, and even about sexual perversions, and even about sexual perversions unknown to those modern university men who write books!

Although often forbidding, Miss Marple can be kind and affectionate. She also has a sense of fun and a twinkle in her eye. In the Caribbean she meets the elderly, disabled Mr Rafiel. They are discussing the murders as though they are detective colleagues. And then Marple teasingly suggests that Mr Rafiel himself might have committed the murders. Rafiel points out that he is too incapacitated to have done so. He goes on to ask who he would wish to murder. Marple responds that she has not yet spoken with him enough to develop a hypothesis about that. Mr Rafiel suggests that talking with Miss Marple is rather dangerous, to which she responds that for someone with a secret conversations are always dangerous.

The varying aspects of Miss Marple's personality have been difficult to capture on screen. Christie dedicates *The Mirror Crack'd from Side to Side* (1962) to Margaret Rutherford. Rutherford had played Miss Marple in four films, the first and best of which was *Murder, She Said*, based on *4.50 from Paddington*. Christie didn't like the films, which were played for laughs and ran roughshod over the plots and characters. Rutherford, however, although hardly tall and thin (which is how Christie describes Marple), conveys the toughness and intelligence whilst also hinting at the fussy manner. Above all, there is a twinkle and a humour in her performances which are a pleasure to watch. Joan Hickson played Mrs Kidder, a cook, in *Murder, She Said*. Twenty years later she was Miss Marple in the BBC TV series. Hickson focusses on Marple's coldness and harshness, conveying also her dithering manner but not the humour, and there is no twinkle in her eyes. Geraldine McEwan, in a more recent TV series, plays up the twittering and the humour and certainly twinkles, but the steely intelligence is lacking. Julia McKenzie, who took over from McEwan in the later episodes, is a good compromise, but although several degrees warmer than Hickson is still rather cold and humourless. Guy Hamilton (famous for *Goldfinger* and several other *Bonds*) directed *The Mirror Crack'd* in 1980 with a cast that included Rock Hudson, Elizabeth Taylor and Tony Curtis. Miss Marple was played by Angela Lansbury, who combines intelligence, ruthlessness and humour – perhaps the best Marple, so far, on screen.

The Mirror Crack'd from Side to Side (1962) has a good example of double dealing. Miss Marple is talking to the police inspector about one of the characters and asks about the children. The inspector replies saying that there was only one child, who has serious brain damage, and is now in a sanatorium. Miss Marple responds by saying that she did not mean that child who sadly did have brain damage through no one's fault. No, she meant the adopted children.

Miss Marple's reply is a major clue, but it also sets the police, the reader and even Miss Marple off in idle pursuit of red herrings.

CHAPTER THIRTY-THREE

Trawling for red herrings

Plots that provide reasons why the innocent may be guilty

No plot spoilers.

When a herring is smoked it acquires a red tinge, and has been known as a red 'heryng' since the fifteenth century. Dogs will follow the scent of a trail laid by dragging a red herring along the ground. By the nineteenth century the phrase 'to draw a red herring across the track' had acquired the metaphorical meaning of attempting to divert attention from the real question.

The key questions in a whodunnit are: who are the perpetrators of the crimes, what are their motives and how were the crimes carried out? A red herring plot is there to divert your attention. It is intended to fool you into thinking that *it* is the central plot. A red herring plot, for example, may provide motive, means or opportunity to do the deed for someone who is, in fact, innocent. Typically those involved in red herring plots have secrets. Red herring plots are usually clued. The purpose of the clues is to lead you, nose following the scent, down the red herring trail, when you believe you are unravelling the main plot.

Red herring plots may serve other purposes. They provide entertainment along the way and add depth to the characters, often giving their back-story, so you can understand why characters may lie about things. In *The Murder on the Links*, you think you are making progress in understanding the main plot only to find out that you have been following a red herring that is revealed well before the end of the book. You feel back at square one, just like playing snakes and ladders and sliding all the way down a slippery snake to the start again! The surprise and frustration are part of the fun.

The revealing of the shoal of red herrings near the end heightens the excitement. Various characters are suspected in turn, and may be accused of being the murderer. This trope is a hallmark of a good Christie mystery in TV adaptations and film take-offs. All the suspects are gathered together in some lovely country-house library. The detective recaps the story so far, points the finger at each suspect in turn before finally revealing the truth. This enjoyable set piece is not so common in Christie novels as is widely supposed. It highlights one of the main problems with red herring plots: the wrong solution can be as plausible as the correct one. Most TV detective stories suffer this problem. Since viewers have too little time to work out a well-clued puzzle, the writers focus less on clues and more on creating red herring dramas.

The Secret of Chimneys (1925) is an early Christie so fizzing with plots and red herrings it is hard to net them all inside the covers of this adventure. Here are the questions Christie asks you to answer:

1. What was Anthony Cade's mysterious past?
2. Who is respectable Virginia Revel's lover?
3. Who murdered Giuseppe? How did they put his body into Mrs Revel's house without any servants noticing?
4. Why try to frame Virginia Revel?
5. What secret, worth killing for, is hidden in Baron Stylptitch's memoirs?
6. Is the body shot in the Council Chamber really Prince Michael of Herzoslovakia?
7. Who shot Prince Michael and why?
8. Why did no one at Chimneys hear the shot in the night?
9. Who is King Victor, the international jewel thief?
10. Where is the fabulously large diamond hidden?
11. Why did the light go on in Mademoiselle Brun's room just after the murder of Prince Michael?
12. Why does Hiram P Fish from New York know nothing about first editions of books?
13. Is this all a Balkan communist plot?

One is dizzy just reading the list. It does make you realise just how complex Christie's novels are. She wove the red herrings in and out of the main plot, so they are difficult to disentangle. For example, the question of the true identity of Anthony Cade is both a red herring throughout the story, and also surprisingly neatly slots into the final solution of the main plot, like the last piece of a jigsaw puzzle. You spend the entire book thinking that Anthony Cade must be King Victor in search of the famous Koh-i-Noor diamond that is hidden somewhere at Chimneys. As Cade himself says every lie leads to further lies and it becomes boring.

Cade is a wonderful, suave, James Bond-like character. When Cade first meets Virginia Revel, she tells him that there is a murdered man in the next room, but what should she do? The dashing, rather surprising response from Cade, who is a complete stranger, is that he has always wanted to get involved in some detective work. Most of us would have said, 'Let's call the police.'

In *Chimneys* very few of the characters are who they say they are. Christie does give clues that are fair, but so much is going on they are easy to miss. *Chimneys* combines thrilling adventure, a whodunnit murder and romance. There are also five detectives! After such an exuberant romp, Christie learned that less is more. She thinned out her detectives to make their thinking easier to follow. She reduced her red herrings to between two and five per book, allowing us to swim through the later novels more easily.

In *Mrs McGinty's Dead*, written almost thirty years after *Chimneys*, Mrs McGinty, a humble charwoman, has been murdered. Her lodger is condemned to death. Christie has used this plot outline before (*Sad Cypress*, *Five Little Pigs*, *Towards Zero*), but the new twist is that the senior police officer, Superintendent Spence, is unhappy, despite all due processes of law having been observed. He pleads with Poirot to investigate. The framing of the lodger is too simplistic, but who else would want to kill a perfectly inoffensive member of the hard-working classes? Poirot unearths a newspaper story about four women who were in some way linked to murders thirty years ago. He knows Mrs McGinty cut out this article just before she died. Christie often used the idea of people adopting differing identities (chapter 8). It provides characters with a secret, and secrets can be used to set up the red herrings. The main plot, and the plots of the red herrings, are that Mrs McGinty must have recognised someone from this newspaper story and that she had been killed to keep her quiet. In the rest of the novel we meet the people Mrs McGinty charred for, piecing together their hidden pasts. We know that most will be red herrings, but *one* has to be the murderer. Except with Christie, all assumptions are off the table. *Mrs McGinty's Dead* has *two* separate murderers in one tiny English village: one for the main plot, and the other in a highly unusual red herring plot. Unusual because in general, in the plots of the red herrings, the crimes, if there are any, are essentially harmless. In this case Poirot is almost killed when, as he is standing on the edge of a railway platform, he is pushed just as the train is approaching. Poirot is saved in the nick of time. He is ecstatic and phones up Superintendent Spence and tells him with great glee that someone has tried to murder him. We share Poirot's jubilation. We must be on the right track at last. But Christie has fooled us. As Poirot discovers, even red kippers can be dangerous. In fact even tumbling to the truth can be dangerous. Near the end of the novel, there is a light-bulb moment for our great detective. He sees it all. He tells Superintendent Spence, in his arrogant, smug way, that the solution is very simple. We are told that there is almost a third murder – the murder of Poirot by Spence. It is fortunate that Superintendent Spence did not kill Poirot, who went on to solve a further nine mysteries.

The last novel that Christie wrote was *Postern of Fate* (1973), published when she was eighty-three years old. The detectives are an aged Tommy and Tuppence, whom we first met in *The Secret Adversary* (1922) when they were young, in love and full of hope. *The Secret Adversary* was published by The Bodley Head, to which Christie was contracted for her first five novels. In 1924 Edmund Cork, Christie's agent, looked to negotiate better terms. It was William Collins that had the foresight to offer the best contract. Christie remained with Collins the rest of her life. The first of Christie's novels that Collins published was *The Murder of Roger Ackroyd* (1926), the novel that set Christie on the road to stardom. In 2013 the Crime Writers' Association voted it the best crime novel ever written.

Christie was soon to have a row with her new publisher when the blurb on the cover identified the murderer. The chairman, Sir Godfrey Collins, sent his nephew, William, known as Billy, who had recently joined the family business, to apologise to Christie in person. Christie was unimpressed that Sir Godfrey himself did not meet with her. Billy, however, was charming. Christie and he hit it off from the start. From then on it was Billy with whom Christie dealt. In 1969 he became chairman of Collins.

Over the years Christie had a few run-ins with Collins,

usually over the blurb on the back of a book or over a cover design – one of which looked as though Poirot was about to have a bath, naked. Billy Collins mollified Christie with presents, including books for her local primary school, hardy rhododendrons, tickets to Wimbledon, a pheasant that melted in the mouth and, in 1953, a car. By this time Christie was Collins' best-selling author. Billy suggested that a Jaguar would be fun but Christie chose the Humber Imperial because it had so much space. And space was more important to her, she wrote, than fun. Thinking of her husband, Max Mallowan, she added that Billy couldn't imagine how much stuff archaeologists carry about with them.

The title Christie chose for her last novel comes from a poem by James Elroy Flecker, 'The Gates of Damascus'. In that poem Flecker describes the East Gate of the city as the 'Postern of Fate'. Those who pass through the gate are doomed to die in the desert. The title has little to do with the novel. Perhaps it was Christie's final clue to her millions of fans that she was seriously unwell.

Christie died on January 12th 1976. At the memorial service at St Martins-in-the-Fields Billy Collins gave an address. But he was himself unwell and died a few months later. Max Mallowan died in August 1978 and is buried with Christie in the churchyard at Cholsey, not far from their house at Wallingford. On the tombstone is written two lines from Edmund Spenser's *Faerie Queen*:

Sleepe after toyle, port after stormy seas
Ease after war, death after life, does greatly please

Further Reading

Earl F Bargainnier (1980) *The Gentle Art of Murder: The Detective Fiction of Agatha Christie* (Wisconsin University Press). This is an entertaining academic book with a focus on character and literary genre rather than her puzzles.

John Curran *Agatha Christie's Secret Notebooks* (2009) and *Agatha Christie's Murder in the Making* (2011), both by HarperCollins. Curran links Christie's notes to her novels.

Three good biographies of Agatha Christie are:

Janet Morgan (1984) *Agatha Christie: A Biography* reprinted in 1997 by HarperCollins.

Laura Thompson (2007) *Agatha Christie: An English Mystery* by Headline Publishing.

Lucy Worsley (2022) *Agatha Christie: A Very Elusive Woman* by Hachette UK (Hodder & Stoughton).

The crime novels of Agatha Christie in chronological order of publication with alternative titles and name of principal detectives

The Mysterious Affair at Styles (1920) Poirot

The Secret Adversary (1922) Tommy and Tuppence

The Murder on the Links (1923) Poirot

The Man in the Brown Suit (1924) Anne Beddingfeld

The Secret of Chimneys (1925) Superintendent Battle

The Murder of Roger Ackroyd (1926) Poirot

The Big Four (1927) Poirot

The Mystery of the Blue Train (1928) Poirot

The Seven Dials Mystery (1929) Superintendent Battle

The Murder at the Vicarage (1930) Marple

The Sittaford Mystery (*The Murder at Hazelmoor*) (1931) Emily Trefusis

Peril at End House (1932) Poirot

Lord Edgware Dies (*Thirteen at Dinner*) (1933) Poirot

Murder on the Orient Express (*Murder in the Calais Coach*) (1934) Poirot

Why Didn't They Ask Evans? (*The Boomerang Clue*) (1934) Bobby Jones and Lady Frances Derwent

Three Act Tragedy (*Murder in Three Acts*) (1934) Poirot

Death in the Clouds (*Death in the Air*) (1935) Poirot

The A.B.C. Murders (1936) Poirot

Murder in Mesopotamia (1936) Poirot

Cards on the Table (1936) Poirot

Dumb Witness (*Poirot Loses a Client*) (1937) Poirot

Death on the Nile (1937) Poirot

Appointment with Death (1938) Poirot

Hercule Poirot's Christmas (*Murder for Christmas*) (1938) Poirot

Murder Is Easy (*Easy to Kill*) (1939) Luke Fitzwilliam, Superintendent Battle

And Then There Were None (1939)

Sad Cypress (1940) Poirot

One, Two, Buckle My Shoe (*The Patriotic Murders*) (1940) Poirot

Evil Under the Sun (1941) Poirot

N or M? (1941) Tommy and Tuppence

The Body in the Library (1942) Marple

Five Little Pigs (*Murder in Retrospect*) (1942) Poirot

The Moving Finger (1942) Marple

Towards Zero (1944) Superintendent Battle

Death Comes as the End (1944) Set in ancient Egypt

Sparkling Cyanide (*Remembered Death*) (1945) Colonel Race and others

The Hollow (1946) Poirot

Taken at the Flood (*There Is a Tide…*) (1948) Poirot

Crooked House (1949) Charles Hayward

A Murder Is Announced (1950) Marple

They Came to Baghdad (1951)

Mrs McGinty's Dead (1952) Poirot

They Do It with Mirrors (*Murder with Mirrors*) (1952) Marple

After the Funeral (*Funerals Are Fatal*) (1953) Poirot

A Pocket Full of Rye (1953) Marple

Destination Unknown (*So Many Steps to Death*) (1954)

Hickory Dickory Dock (*Hickory Dickory Death*) (1955) Poirot

Dead Man's Folly (1956) Poirot

4.50 from Paddington (*What Mrs McGillicuddy Saw!*) (1957) Marple

Ordeal by Innocence (1958) Arthur Calgary

Cat Among the Pigeons (1959) Poirot

The Pale Horse (1961) Mark Easterbrook

The Mirror Crack'd from Side to Side (*The Mirror Crack'd*) (1962) Marple

The Clocks (1963) Poirot

A Caribbean Mystery (1964) Marple

At Bertram's Hotel (1965) Marple

Third Girl (1966) Poirot

Endless Night (1967)

By the Pricking of My Thumbs (1968) Tommy and Tuppence

Hallowe'en Party (1969) Poirot

Passenger to Frankfurt (1970)

Nemesis (1971) Marple

Elephants Can Remember (1972) Poirot

Postern of Fate (1973) Tommy and Tuppence

Curtain (1975) Poirot

Sleeping Murder (1976) Marple

About the Authors

Sally and Tony Hope are retired medical doctors who have enjoyed Agatha Christie novels for over forty years. They were trained to understand and interpret the clues that lead to diagnosis and treatment. They have applied that training to the solving of Agatha Christie's crime novels.

Tony Hope

Tony was a psychiatrist and the first Professor of Medical Ethics at the University of Oxford. He was co-author of the first four editions of *The Oxford Handbook of Clinical Medicine*. He has co-authored a self-help book of practical psychology (*Manage Your Mind*) as well as books on medical ethics and medical law. He is an Emeritus Fellow of St Cross College, and an Honorary Fellow of New College, Oxford.

Sally Hope

Sally was a general practitioner for thirty-two years with a special interest in women's health. She was the regular doctor on a weekly radio phone-in programme on BBC Radio Oxford for many years and also a guest on *Woman's Hour*. She was medical columnist for *Best* magazine for six years. Sally has co-authored and edited a number of books for general practitioners, including *The Oxford Handbook of Clinical Genetics*.

Internet presence of the authors:

https://poirotscore.com
https://www.theoldie.co.uk/blog/queen-of-crime-agatha-christie